LIVING IN GOD'S
ABUNDANCE

LIVING IN GOD'S ABUNDANCE

by

Billy Joe Daugherty

Living in God's Abundance
ISBN 1-56267-184-7
Copyright © 1998 by·
Billy Joe Daugherty
Victory Christian Center
7700 South Lewis Avenue
Tulsa, OK 74136

CONTENTS

Contents

INTRODUCTION

To live in God's abundance means different things to different people. To some it means healing and wholeness. To others it means a fluency in their finances. An area of abundance in my life is the freedom to be a soulwinner for Jesus Christ, sharing Him with people of all ages from one end of the earth to the other.

To a teacher in one of Tulsa's elementary schools, living in abundance means to have a "Reading Day," a creative idea, where she invites professional people to come to the school and read to the children from their favorite book. If you invite the right people, the children can enjoy a lot of good reading material.

On Good Friday I spoke in two of the fourth grade classes in this elementary school. Since the Bible is my favorite book, I began to ask the children some questions: "What day is it?" They responded, "It's Good Friday." "What happened on Good Friday?" I asked. One little boy said, "Jesus was crucified." Then I asked, "What happened after that?" "He was raised from the dead," the same little boy responded. Another little boy said, "They stuck Jesus in a hole and He popped out!" The same boy answered most of the questions and shared the Word of God with his classmates. The students said, "He's going to be a preacher."

We prayed and I gave an altar call. Several fourth graders, as well as many other children in that elementary school, received Jesus Christ as their Lord and Savior that day. It was obvious that the principal and many of the teachers loved the Lord. I call that God's abundance — God using the gift and anointing upon a public schoolteacher to bring an influence of righteousness into her entire school.

God's abundance to Dr. Jimmy Buskirk, former Dean of Oral Roberts University's Seminary and now senior pastor at First United Methodist Church in downtown Tulsa, meant a supernatural miracle of healing. He faced a severe physical challenge years ago when he first began pastoring.

Dr. Buskirk was losing his eyesight and didn't want anyone but his wife to know, so he memorized the steps on the platform to the podium to preach. He worked with his wife to memorize his sermons. He had his Bible and some notes, but he memorized the verses. As a young preacher, he was struggling because his whole future was ahead of him and he had many dreams.

Sometime later when he told his father what was happening, he made an appointment at a famous medical center where he and his son would go. His intent was to give his eyes to his son, Dr. Buskirk, through a surgical procedure.

Dr. Buskirk said, "The moment he spoke that, I began to have a revelation. If my earthly father loved me that much, how much more did my heavenly Father love me?" When he got a revelation of the love of God, faith arose in his heart and he received a supernatural healing. His vision was fully restored by the power of God over a period of time.

Restoration is a part of living in abundance. Your joy and peace levels are part of living in abundance. It also includes the salvation of your children and physical, emotional and financial well-being.

If you have a need for healing, part of the healing process is getting a revelation of how much Jesus loves you. Once you realize His love for you, your spirit will open up for a miracle of healing to come inside of you.

Provision is a key part of abundant living. Scott and Marla Schiele, directors of Camp Victory, were compacted together in a trailer home with three small children and their office. They began believing God and confessing by faith that God would provide a log cabin for their housing, to fit in with the decor of the camp.

One day while driving down Lewis Avenue in Tulsa, I noticed a mailing business located in a log cabin which had just been closed. The thought came to me, "The owner might want to give the building away. They would give it to Camp Victory."

I talked with one of our staff members, Bruce Edwards, and he in turn talked with the owner. As a result, the log cabin was given to Victory Christian Center. The home that Scott and Marla seeded for has now become a reality. It has been moved out to Camp Victory for their new home.

Seed planting works and God wants His people blessed. That's part of His plan of living in abundance.

In this book, *Living in God's Abundance*, we'll examine Scriptures to find out how Abraham, the father of our faith, received the blessing of God of which we are now joint-heirs with Jesus Christ. We will look at our redemption from the curse and gain an understanding of the provision God has already made for us. We'll lift the lid off a poverty and lack mentality and attempt to gain an understanding of God's will for us to enjoy abundant living. We'll look at God's avenue of increase — seedtime and harvest — and the importance of aligning our thoughts and words with what God says about His plan for our prosperity. We'll look at giving with an expectation to receive the hundredfold return in the same year that seed is planted.

If you are ready to move into God's abundance and be increased more and more for the purpose of being a blessing in the earth — sharing the Gospel of Jesus Christ with others — then this book is for you! Read on with an expectation of increase which will come as you commit to an increase in your giving. My prayer for you is in agreement with Psalm 115:14: **"May the Lord give you increase more and more, you and your children."**

Billy Joe Daugherty

CHAPTER 1
REDEEMED FROM THE CURSE

When Jesus died on the cross and gave His blood for us, He took our sin and the penalty for it. He redeemed us. That means He purchased us, and in that purchase He freed us from the curse of the law.

Galatians 3:13,14,26-29 speaks of our freedom from the curse of the law:

> Christ has redeemed us from the curse of the law, having become a curse for us (for it is written, "Cursed is everyone who hangs on a tree"),
>
> That the blessing of Abraham might come upon the Gentiles in Christ Jesus, that we might receive the promise of the Spirit through faith.
>
> For you are all sons of God through faith in Christ Jesus.
>
> For as many of you as were baptized into Christ have put on Christ.
>
> There is neither Jew nor Greek, there is neither slave nor free, there is neither male nor female; for you are all one in Christ Jesus.
>
> And if you are Christ's, then you are Abraham's seed, and heirs according to the promise.

When I was growing up, we never talked much about Abraham. In fact, I really didn't know who Abraham was. I barely knew who Noah was. When I came to Oral Roberts University, I found out who Abraham, Isaac and Jacob were in my Old Testament Survey Class.

Later I heard the song, "Abraham's Blessings Are Mine," and I began to wonder, "What does this mean? What is this curse? What is it all about?"

1

To be redeemed from the curse means to be purchased and released, as a kidnapped person who has a ransom price paid for their release. We had been sold into slavery and trapped in sin and in the bondage of Satan. Jesus paid the price for our sin, and now we're liberated, set free, released, delivered from the bondage of the curse and sin's consequences. The price has been paid in full, but individually we must make the choice to accept or reject this freedom.

We don't have to experience the penalties for our sin. It is through faith in Jesus Christ that we become sons of God (Galatians 3:26). This is the Gospel of Jesus Christ.

Now that we are sons, we have become Abraham's seed because Jesus was *the* seed of Abraham. When we receive Him into our life, then that same blessing that was promised to Abraham and his seed comes on us. Paul uses the phraseology, **"...heirs of God and joint heirs with Christ"** (Romans 8:17).

Heirs of God

Romans 8:16,17 says:
The Spirit Himself bears witness with our spirit that we are children of God,

And if children, then heirs — heirs of God and joint heirs with Christ, if indeed we suffer with Him, that we may also be glorified together.

Hebrews 2:11 says Jesus is not ashamed to call us brethren. Why? Because we have the same Father He has. We are in the same family. By grace we have now become heirs. There is nothing we can do in ourselves to earn it, and the right standing we have with God is through faith in Jesus Christ.

Few people really appreciate the promises they inherit as children of God until they understand the depth of the curses as well as the depth of the blessings which God provided.

The curse of the law is explained in Deuteronomy

28:15-68. It affects every aspect of man's existence — spirit, soul, body, family and finances.

Jesus took the curse for those who accept Him as their Lord and Savior and are obedient to His Word. We have been legally freed from the curse through Jesus' shed blood. This means the curse has no legal right to come upon your life once you are born again. It also means that as God's children, the blessings God promised to Abraham and to his descendants belong to you and me.

Verse 29 of Galatians, chapter 3, says, **"And if you are Christ's, then you are Abraham's seed, and heirs according to the promise."** An "heir" is a person who has a right to an inheritance by reason of *relationship*. Maybe the heir is a friend, an aunt or uncle, a niece or nephew, a child or a grandchild, but there is some type of relationship to the person who wrote a will and identified the inheritance they are to receive.

By faith in Christ, we are heirs in this life of the blessings God spoke to Abraham. We don't have to live under the curse anymore. The eternal, final consequences of it — hell, the lake of fire, separation from God forever — are removed from us.

The curse comes as a consequence of breaking the laws of God. It includes guilt, shame, torment, condemnation, fear, oppression, sickness, disease, destruction, poverty, divorce and rebellion in the home. That's only part of the curse. Many people, because they don't know what the curse is, even though they are Christians, tolerate the curse in their life. It's time that you know the difference between the blessings and the curses so you can choose the blessings and say "no" to the curses.

Unless you make a decision that you are going to resist the source of the curses, Satan, that liar, thief, killer and destroyer will try to sell you a bill of goods that what has happened in your life is God's will. If you don't know the difference between the blessings and the curses, you'll just say, "Well, I guess this is God's will. Whatever will be will be." Get it straight!

The blessing is opposite of the curse. God wants you blessed, not cursed.

Let's look at this great difference in our own lives. Let me give you a little picture. The country of Haiti is just an hour and a half from Miami by air, in the middle of the Caribbean. It is the poorest country in the Western Hemisphere. Many years ago, a group of leaders in that country sacrificed animals and dedicated part of the island to the devil. Voodoo was announced by the leadership of Haiti as a national, cultural expression of their nation. I'm talking about witchcraft — worshipping the devil. When you do that, you are not going to be blessed.

All around Haiti are islands that are far more blessed than they are. Haiti doesn't lack in natural resources, but they lack in the blessings of God. When you go there and see the devastation in homes and families all around you, you feel like, "This is the curse personified in every way."

Recently Haitian Christian leaders met and went to the exact same spot where that curse had been pronounced and they broke it. They have dedicated their island to God, and Haiti will see a turnaround. No longer is voodoo proclaimed as a national, cultural expression of their nation by their leadership, but there's a change taking place.

Until people recognize the Source and cause of the blessing and the source and cause of the curse and begin to change their views, conditions will remain the same. It is God's will that you be blessed.

Identifying Some of the Curses

Many people are quick to shout, "Jesus redeemed me," but few realize the curses they have been redeemed from. Jesus became a curse for you so you wouldn't have to experience the curses as a consequence for your sin. Jesus took your penalty. He took your pain, hurt and torment. That's the Good News of the Gospel of Jesus Christ. When you realize what Jesus did so you could be blessed, you will love Him more than you've ever loved Him in your whole life.

In the natural, there are consequences for breaking the law, such as speeding. In the spiritual realm, there are consequences or penalties for breaking or disobeying God's laws. Let's look at some of these penalties or curses listed in Deuteronomy 28:15-68:

> **But it shall come to pass, if you do not obey the voice of the Lord your God, to observe carefully all His commandments and His statutes which I command you today, that all these curses will come upon you and overtake you:**
>
> **Cursed shall you be in the city, and cursed shall you be in the country.**
>
> **Cursed shall be your basket and your kneading bowl.** [This has to do with your food supply.]
>
> **Cursed shall be the fruit of your body....** [That's your children. They'll not honor God or be righteous and holy, or be a blessing.] **...and the produce of your land** [your crops], **the increase of your cattle and the offspring of your flocks.**
>
> **Cursed shall you be when you come in, and cursed shall you be when you go out.** [It doesn't matter which direction you are going, evil and calamity will follow you.]
>
> **The Lord will send on you cursing, confusion, and rebuke in all you set your hand to do, until you are destroyed and until you perish quickly, because of the wickedness of your doings in which you have forsaken Me.** [He is saying, if you do wrong and you forsake the Lord, then these curses will come.]
>
> **The Lord will make the plague cling to you until He has consumed you from the land which you are going to possess.**
>
> **Verses 15-21**

Years ago in America, medical experts announced that major diseases would be destroyed because of all the miracle drugs and modern medicine. Yet today there are strains of germs and diseases that are resistant to antibiotics. Tuberculosis has had a resurgence in our country. It's time for us to get on God's Word, because the Spirit of God through Moses speaks of a curse that will cling and not be removed.

> **The Lord will strike you with consumption, with fever, with inflammation, with severe burning fever, with the sword, with scorching, and with mildew; they shall pursue you until you perish.**
>
> **And your heavens which are over your head shall be bronze, and the earth which is under you shall be iron.** [That means no rain, no harvest, no crops, famine and lack of food.]
>
> **The Lord will change the rain of your land to powder and dust; from the heaven it shall come down on you until you are destroyed.**
>
> **The Lord will cause you to be defeated before your enemies; you will go out one way against them and flee seven ways before them; you will become troublesome to all the kingdoms of the earth.**
>
> **Your carcasses shall be food for all the birds of the air and the beasts of the earth, and no one shall frighten them away.**
>
> **The Lord will strike you with the boils of Egypt, with tumors, with the scab, and with the itch, from which you cannot be healed.**
>
> **The Lord will strike you with madness and blindness and confusion of heart.**
>
> **Verses 22-28**

Right now America's psychiatric treatment centers are over-flowing because of madness, insanity and instability of the mind that people are experiencing as a result of what has happened to them. Yet, God's promise to His children is, "I have not given you a spirit of fear, but of power, love and a *sound mind*" (2 Timothy 1:7).

And you shall grope at noonday, as a blind man gropes in darkness; you shall not prosper in your ways; you shall be only oppressed and plundered continually, and no one shall save you.

Verse 29

To fail to prosper in your ways means you will not receive God's blessings, and you won't experience joy and peace.

You shall betroth [marry] **a wife, but another man shall lie with her** [infidelity]; **you shall build a house, but you shall not dwell in it; you shall plant a vineyard, but you shall not gather its grapes.** [You will invest your life in a work, but someone else will reap the harvest or benefits of it.]

Your ox shall be slaughtered before your eyes, but you shall not eat of it; your donkey shall be violently taken away from before you [that could be a Chevy or a Ford!], **and shall not be restored to you; your sheep shall be given to your enemies, and you shall have no one to rescue them.**

Your sons and your daughters shall be given to another people, and your eyes shall look and fail with longing for them all day long; and there will be no strength in your hand.

Verses 30-32

Just as the children of Israel looked for their sons and daughters but they were in captivity, many people today are looking for their sons and daughters, some of them runaways, who are in captivity to drugs, alcohol, immorality and uncleanness.

A nation whom you have not known shall eat the fruit of your land and the produce of your labor, and you shall be only oppressed and crushed continually.

So you shall be driven mad because of the sight which your eyes see.

The Lord will strike you in the knees and on the legs with severe boils which cannot be healed, and from the sole of your foot to the top of your head.

The Lord will bring you and the king whom you set over you to a nation which neither you nor your fathers have known, and there you will serve other gods — wood and stone.

And you will become an astonishment, a proverb, and a byword among all nations where the Lord will drive you.

You shall carry much seed out to the field but gather little in, for the locust shall consume it.

You shall plant vineyards and tend them, but you shall neither drink of the wine nor gather the grapes; for the worms shall eat them. [Inflation!]

You shall have olive trees throughout all your territory, but you shall not anoint yourself with the oil; for your olives shall drop off.

You shall beget sons and daughters, but they shall not be yours; for they shall go into captivity.

Locusts shall consume all your trees and the produce of your land.

The alien who is among you shall rise higher and higher above you, and you shall come down lower and lower.

He shall lend to you, but you shall not lend to him; he shall be the head, and you shall be the tail.

Verses 33-44

This is talking about lending and borrowing. When you are the borrower, you are the tail. Many Christians don't know the difference between the blessing and the curse. They are living in the curse thinking, "This is just normal." It is *not* normal, according to God's Word, to be in debt. There must come a righteous indignation when you finally read the truth and say, "Are you telling me if I am in debt, I am the tail?" Exactly! God doesn't want you to be the tail anymore. It's time to make a decision, "I'm coming off the bottom and I'm going to the top." You've got to know it first, then believe it, start declaring it and acting on it by faith.

**Moreover all these curses shall come upon you and
pursue and overtake you, until you are destroyed, because
you did not obey the voice of the Lord your God, to keep
His commandments and His statutes which He
commanded you.** [*Disobedience* is the open door to the
curse.]

**And they shall be upon you for a sign and a wonder,
and on your descendants forever.**

Verses 45,46

Verse 47 gives another condition that allows the curse to
come on people: **"Because you did not serve the Lord your
God *with joy and gladness of heart*, for the abundance of
everything."**

It is God's desire that we not only have everything we need,
but that we have an abundance of it. But He expects us to serve
Him with joy and gladness. He wants a *relationship* where we
express our love for Him and are appreciative of all the things
He has given us and has done for us.

We take so many things for granted. In America we meet
in air-conditioned buildings. But in Zimbabwe, there is no air-
conditioning. You are sweating in 110 or 120 degree weather,
with thousands of people packed in for meetings.

There are twenty-one more verses of the curse, verses
48-68, which include being taken captive by the enemy, other
people enjoying the fruit of the increase while the disobedient
are in famine, plagues and sicknesses, fear and despair.

Let's not shortchange Calvary again, but let's rejoice that
Jesus took our curse so we could enjoy His blessings. To move
from the curses to the blessings, you need to be born again. And
if you are born again but you are doing your own thing, you
need to repent. In either case, it's time to get right. Pray with
me right now:

*Father, I repent of all sin and of disobedience to the truth of
Your Word. I have heard enough of the curses to know they're
not for me!*

9

I believe Jesus Christ is Your Son and that He gave His blood at Calvary to pay the penalty in full for my sin and disobedience. I receive You now, Jesus, as my Lord and Savior. I yield to Your lordship in my life.

I acknowledge You, Lord, as the Potter and myself as the clay (Jeremiah 18:6). Mold me daily as You will, Lord, so that I continually mature into Your image and likeness.

Empower me with Your Spirit, Lord, so I will be a bold witness of You, drawing others out of the world of darkness, confusion and turmoil of a cursed lifestyle, into one of light and blessings in You, Lord Jesus. Amen.

Abundant Living Confessions

Here are five Abundant Living Personalized Confessions from Chapter 1, which will help to move you into the mainstream of God's abundance:

1. As a born-again believer, I have been redeemed from the curse of the law because of Jesus' shed blood and completed work at Calvary (Galatians 3:13,14).
2. Because I am Christ's, I am Abraham's seed and an heir of all the promises God gave to Abraham (Galatians 3:29).
3. By my acceptance of Jesus' shed blood, I am released from the bondage of sin and its consequences.
4. I am an heir of God and a joint heir with Christ (Romans 8:17).
5. The curse comes as a consequence for breaking (or disobeying) the laws of God. I will walk in obedience to God's Word and thereby come into agreement with God's will for me to be blessed in every area of my life.

CHAPTER 2

REDEEMED INTO GOD'S BLESSINGS

O nce Moses had laid out all of the blessings and curses, he said, **"...I have set before you life and death, blessing and cursing; therefore** *choose life,* **that both you and your descendants may live"** (Deuteronomy 30:19). I want to encourage you, choose to obey so you can enjoy God's blessings every day.

Deuteronomy 28:1-14 explains what we have been redeemed to — the blessings of God. To be *blessed* means to be enriched, prospered, increased, fulfilled, favored, rewarded and satisfied.

> **Now it shall come to pass, if you diligently** *obey* **the voice of the Lord your God, to observe carefully all His commandments which I command you today, that the Lord your God will set you high above all nations of the earth.**
>
> **And all these blessings shall come upon you and overtake you, because you obey the voice of the Lord your God:**
>
> **Blessed shall you be in the city, and blessed shall you be in the country.**
>
> **Blessed shall be the fruit of your body, the produce of your ground and the increase of your herds, the increase of your cattle and the offspring of your flocks.**
>
> **Verses 1-4**

The two main sources of income were crops and livestock. Yours could be real estate investments or your job.

> **Blessed shall be your basket and your kneading bowl** [your food supply].

> **Blessed shall you be when you come in, and blessed shall you be when you go out.**
>
> **The Lord will cause your enemies who rise against you to be defeated before your face; they shall come out against you one way and flee before you seven ways.**
>
> **The Lord will command the blessing on you in your storehouses and in all to which you set your hand, and He will bless you in the land which the Lord your God is giving you.**
>
> **Verses 5-8**

In other words, everything you touch, every investment you make, every job you hold, will prosper. You will succeed and increase, and it will bring satisfaction and fulfillment.

Proverbs 10:22 says, **"The blessing of the Lord makes one rich, and He adds no sorrow with it."** Many people in the world have wealth, but they also have pain, brokenness and torment. You can't have peace in your life unless you have *peace with God*, so although you may have lots of material possessions, you may have little or no peace. The blessing of the Lord touches your spirit, soul, body, family and finances — every area of your life. Make a decision that you are going to walk in God's blessings.

Verse 9 of Deuteronomy, chapter 28, says:

> **The Lord will establish you as a holy people to Himself, just as He has sworn to you, if you keep the commandments of the Lord your God and walk in His ways.**

This means to be delivered from wickedness, sinfulness, unrighteousness and unholiness.

The two greatest commandments of the New Testament are:

> **"You shall love the Lord your God with all your heart, with all your soul, and with all your mind." This is the first and great commandment. And the second is like it: "You shall love your neighbor as yourself."**
>
> **Matthew 22:37-39**

If we love God with all of our heart (loving God means obeying Him) and we love our neighbor as ourself, we will keep the commandments. In the New Covenant, when we walk by love — loving God first and then our neighbor — we step into the place of blessing.

Let's go on with the blessings of Deuteronomy, chapter 28:

Then all peoples of the earth shall see that you are called by the name of the Lord, and they shall be afraid of you.

And the Lord will grant you plenty of goods, in the fruit of your body, in the increase of your livestock, and in the produce of your ground [whatever type of work you are doing]**, and in the land of which the Lord swore to your fathers to give you.**

The Lord will open to you His good treasure, the heavens, to give the rain to your land in its season, and to bless all the work of your hand. You shall lend to many nations, but you shall not borrow.

Verses 10-12

How would you like to be on the giving end where you are reaping a hundredfold harvest on every seed that you sow? That is God's kind of abundance. He wants you to be blessed so you can bless other nations with the Gospel.

A woman in our congregation who was in her sixties, Alice Bush, was in a wheelchair. She believed in the blessings of Abraham and divine healing. She walked right out of her wheelchair onto the mission field! Now, in her late seventies, she's still preaching Jesus in the nations of the earth. Why? Because she got hold of the blessing of God. She said of her circumstances, "This is the curse. This isn't the blessing. I'm going to believe for the blessing." She still has something she can do to help other people.

And the Lord will make you the head and not the tail; you shall be above only, and not be beneath, if you

**heed the commandments of the Lord your God, which I
command you today, and are careful to observe them.**

**So you shall not turn aside from any of the words
which I command you this day, to the right or the left, to
go after other gods to serve them.**

Verses 13,14

For many people, these blessings are so good they think, "It
couldn't be that good." It is! This is the Gospel of Jesus Christ.

In Luke, chapter 4, Jesus opened the book of Isaiah and
read:

**"The Spirit of the Lord is upon Me, because He has
anointed Me to preach the gospel to the poor; He has
sent Me to heal the brokenhearted, to proclaim liberty to
the captives and recovery of sight to the blind, to set at
liberty those who are oppressed;**

"To proclaim the acceptable year of the Lord."

Verses 18,19

Jesus came to set us free from the curse. The "acceptable
year of the Lord" refers to the year of Jubilee when your crops,
your flocks and your businesses are going to prosper. I am
telling you, the Gospel includes *everything that involves your
life*. The forgiveness of your sin is the most important, but God
didn't stop there. He paid a price through His Son's death so
you could have all the blessings that He promised to Abraham.
It's time to take a stand and believe it with all of your heart.
When you believe it, you will begin to declare it and resist
the curse.

In John 10:10, Jesus simply restated Deuteronomy 28: **"The
thief** [the devil] **does not come except to steal, and to kill,
and to destroy. I have come that they may have life, and that
they may have it more abundantly."**

The devil has come to bring the curse, but Jesus came to
bring God's blessings. Your greatest resistance to the curse is
obedience to God and to His Word.

The Israelites didn't declare their blessings. Instead of being grateful, they murmured and complained:

> **Ye have said, It is vain to serve God: and what profit is it that we have kept his ordinance, and that we have walked mournfully before the Lord of hosts?**
>
> **And now we call the proud happy; yea, they that work wickedness are set up; yea, they that tempt God are even delivered.**
>
> Malachi 3:14,15 KJV

God said, **"Your words have been stout against me..."** (v. 13 KJV). The Israelites were saying, "Those who serve the Lord don't get blessed, but those who are wicked prosper." God said:

> **Ye are cursed with a curse: for ye have robbed me, even this whole nation.**
>
> **Bring ye all the tithes into the storehouse, that there may be meat in mine house, and prove me now herewith, saith the Lord of hosts, if I will not open you the windows of heaven, and pour you out a blessing, that there shall not be room enough to receive it.**
>
> **And I will rebuke the devourer for your sakes, and he shall not destroy the fruits of your ground; neither shall your vine cast her fruit before the time in the field, saith the Lord of hosts.**
>
> **And all nations shall call you blessed: for ye shall be a delightsome land, saith the Lord of hosts.**
>
> Malachi 3:9-12 KJV

God is saying, "I'm going to open heaven for those who will obey My voice." Malachi was just repeating the blessing of Abraham.

In Malachi, God said, **"I will rebuke the devourer"** (v. 11). In Deuteronomy 28:7 He said, "Though the enemy comes against you one way, I will cause him to flee from you seven ways. I will stop the devil from stealing your children. I will stop him from stealing your goods, taking the things that I have blessed you with. I will rebuke him Myself, and I will do it for your sake." Why? "Because I have made a promise to Abraham that in blessing I would bless him, and in multiplying I would multiply him. [This covenant promise is also for you and me today.] If you meet My conditions, I will open the windows of heaven and pour blessings out upon your life."

Abundant Living Confessions

Here are fourteen Abundant Living Personalized Confessions from Chapter 2, which will help to move you into the mainstream of God's abundance:

1. To be "abundantly" blessed, I will diligently obey the voice of the Lord and the commandments of His Word.
2. God is the Source of *all* of my abundance.
3. I am increasing and succeeding in all that God has called me to do.
4. My checking and savings accounts are blessed, in Jesus' name.
5. My children are blessed.
6. God's blessings make me rich, and He adds no sorrow with it (Proverbs 10:22).
7. God's peace rules in my heart and life.
8. I love the Lord my God with all my heart and mind, and I love my neighbor as myself (Matthew 22:37-39).
9. To love God means that I am quick to obey Him.
10. I am a lender, not a borrower (Deuteronomy 28:12).
11. I am the head and not the tail, above and not beneath (Deuteronomy 28:13).
12. The devil is out to steal, kill and destroy, but Jesus has come to give me life and life more abundantly (John 10:10).

13. My tithe (10 percent of my gross income) belongs to the storehouse (church) where I attend and am fed spiritually (Malachi 3:10).
14. As a tither, God promises to rebuke the devourer (Satan) and open the windows of heaven and pour me out a blessing there is not room enough to receive. Abundance! (Malachi 3:10,11).

CHAPTER 3
THE ABRAHAMIC COVENANT

The blessing of Abraham comes through faith in Jesus Christ. If we believe in Christ, we are heirs to the same promises that God made to Abraham. So how did the "blessing of Abraham" come about? Let's look at portions of Scripture from Genesis to learn more about this man, Abram, who later became Abraham.

> Now the Lord had said to Abram: "Get out of your country, from your family and from your father's house, to a land that I will show you.
>
> "I will make you a great nation; I will bless you and make your name great; and *you shall be a blessing.*
>
> "I will bless those who bless you, and I will curse him who curses you; and in you all the families of the earth shall be blessed."
>
> **Genesis 12:1-3**

The next verse gives us one of the conditions Abram met that caused him to be blessed by God: **"So Abram departed *as the Lord had spoken to him...*"** (v. 4). In other words, he was quick to obey the Lord to get out of his own country and to go to a land God chose for him and his family.

Lot, the son of Abram's brother Haran, traveled with Abram. Lot had no inheritance in that land, but he, by his own choice, followed Abram.

Genesis, chapter 13, verse 2 says, **"Abram was very rich in livestock, in silver, and in gold."** God blessed Abram's flocks so much that his possessions and Lot's were too great to continue to dwell together.

> Now the land was not able to support them, that they
> might dwell together, for their possessions were so great
> that they could not dwell together.
>
> **Genesis 13:6**

As a result, Abram and Lot's herdsmen got into strife. When
Abram heard about the strife, he said to Lot:

> **"Please let there be no strife between you and me,
> and between my herdsmen and your herdsmen; for we
> are brethren.**
>
> **"Is not the whole land before you? Please separate
> from me. If you take the left, then I will go to the right;
> or, if you go to the right, then I will go to the left."**
>
> **Genesis 13:8,9**

Abram was willing to give up and let go of what appeared
to be the "best" of the land. Why? When you know who your
Father is, you are not bothered by real estate or material things.

Abram told Lot to take what he wanted and he would go the
opposite direction so there would be no strife. Lot chose what
looked like the best of the land. Once Abram was separated
from Lot, the Lord spoke to him:

> **"Lift your eyes now and look from the place where
> you are — northward, southward, eastward, and
> westward;**
>
> **"For all the land which you see I give to you and your
> descendants forever.**
>
> **"And I will make your descendants as the dust of the
> earth; so that if a man could number the dust of the earth,
> then your descendants also could be numbered.**
>
> **"Arise, walk in the land through its length and its
> width, for I give it to you."**
>
> **Genesis 13:14-17**

God will override the decisions of people to get His blessings to His children. If you are involved in strife over financial
or legal situations or over an inheritance, go over the heads of
those involved to the Judge Himself. I'm talking about the Judge
of the whole earth. Why mess with any lower court? Just go to

the top. Put it in God's hands. You say, "What if they choose the best?" That's what Lot got, he thought, until God said, "It belongs to Abraham."

If you have faith in Jesus Christ and you have accepted Him as your Lord and Savior, then the blessings of Abraham are available to you. That means you don't have to get into strife and fight with people over "things." God will bring His abundance to you in His time. Ecclesiastes 3:11 says, **"He has made everything beautiful in its time."** *In due season God will exalt you to possess the land He has promised you.*

In Genesis, chapter 14, Abram went down to the area of Sodom and Gomorrah to rescue Lot who had been taken captive by enemy armies, along with his goods, other people and their goods. Abram took 318 armed servants with him and went after them. They recovered *everything*. As they returned, Abram met Melchizedek the king of Salem. Scripture says:

> **Then Melchizedek king of Salem brought out bread and wine; he was the priest of God Most High.**
> **And he blessed him and said: "Blessed be Abram of God Most High, Possessor of heaven and earth;**
> **"And blessed be God Most High, Who has delivered your enemies into your hand." And he** [Abram] **gave him** [Melchizedek] **a tithe of all.**
>
> **Genesis 14:18-20**

One of the blessings of Abraham is a *relationship* with the God Who owns heaven and earth. To understand the importance of the tithe, even before it became law, denotes a viable relationship. When Abraham went out to fight, he didn't lose one man. He recovered all. God's will is that we not lose one battle, but that we be delivered from all of the works of the devil.

Abram Acknowledged God as Owner of *All*

The tithe was given in recognition that God is the possessor and owner of *all* things. Everything we have is God's. We are simply stewards of it.

21

> **Now the king of Sodom said to Abram, "Give me the persons, and take the goods for yourself."**
> **But Abram said to the king of Sodom, "I have raised my hand to the Lord, God Most High, the Possessor of heaven and earth."**
>
> **Verses 21,22**

When did Abram raise his hand to the Lord? When he gave his tithe and offering. He was saying, "I have come into relationship with the Most High God — the God Who owns it all. I've brought my tithe and offering to Him."

> **"That I will take nothing, from a thread to a sandal strap, and that I will not take anything that is yours, lest you should say, 'I have made Abram rich.' "**
>
> **Genesis 14:23**

Abram was saying, "God is my Source. I don't want anyone except God to get credit for the riches that are in my life. God has given them *all* to me." Like Abram, God is the Source of *all* that has been entrusted to us, whether it is ministry gifts, talents, material goods, or financial provision.

God Explains His Covenant With Abraham

> **When Abram was ninety-nine years old, the Lord appeared to Abram and said to him, "I am Almighty God; walk before Me and be blameless."**
>
> **Genesis 17:1**

Almighty God means "El Shaddai," the all-sufficient God, the God Who is more than enough, the God of abundant provision, the God Who has everything that you need, the God of ample, plentiful, bountiful supply.

> **And I will make My covenant between Me and you, and will multiply you exceedingly.**
>
> **Genesis 17:2**

Abram fell on his face before God, and God began to explain the covenant to him:

22

"As for Me, behold, My covenant is with you, and you shall be a father of many nations.

"No longer shall your name be called Abram, but your name shall be Abraham; for I have made you a father of many nations.

"I will make you exceedingly fruitful...."

Genesis 17:4-6

We are to be fruitful. This sounds like John, chapter 15, verses 5 and 16, where Jesus said:

"I am the vine, you are the branches. He who abides in Me, and I in him, bears much fruit.... You did not choose Me, but I chose you and appointed you that you should go and bear fruit, and that your fruit should remain...."

In Genesis, chapter 17, God continues to speak to Abram:

"...I will make nations of you, and kings shall come from you.

"And I will establish My covenant between Me and you and your descendants after you in their generations, for an everlasting covenant, to be God to you and your descendants after you."

Genesis 17:6,7

We pick up on the word *descendants* in the New Testament as "seed" or "Abraham's seed." God's covenant was not only with Abraham, but with all those born into his lineage. That includes you and me. Galatians 3:29 says, **"And if you are Christ's, then you are *Abraham's seed*, and heirs according to the promise."**

Abraham got into the covenant by faith. The entire book of Galatians is on the subject of faith versus works. When you believe God and act in faith, you get in on the same blessings that belonged to Abraham. You are grafted into the covenant when you yield to the lordship of Jesus Christ.

God continues to explain the covenant to Abram:

"Also I give to you and your descendants after you the land in which you are a stranger, all the land of

Canaan, as an everlasting possession; and I will be their God."

And God said to Abraham: "As for you, you shall keep My covenant, you and your descendants after you throughout their generations.

"This is My covenant which you shall keep, between Me and you and your descendants after you: Every male child among you shall be circumcised."

Genesis 17:8-10

While male circumcision was an outward sign of the Old Covenant, in the New Covenant God cuts away the work of the flesh in our hearts and puts a new spirit within us. Our circumcision is of the heart, where He removes the old nature of sin and puts in a new nature of righteousness when we have faith in Christ and are born again. Then the life of God comes inside of us.

The prophet Ezekiel spoke of this in Ezekiel 11:19,20 KJV:

And I will give them one heart, and I will put a new spirit within you; and I will take the stony heart out of their flesh, and will give them an heart of flesh:

That they may walk in my statutes, and keep mine ordinances, and do them: and they shall be my people, and I will be their God.

Covenant Benefits

One aspect of the Abrahamic covenant is that *God will reveal to you things to come*. When God was about to destroy Sodom and Gomorrah, He said:

"Shall I hide from Abraham what I am doing,

"Since Abraham shall surely become a great and mighty nation, and all the nations of the earth shall be blessed in him?

"For I have known him, in order that he may command his children and his household after him, that they keep the way of the Lord, to do righteousness and

justice, that the Lord may bring to Abraham what He has spoken to him."

Genesis 18:17-19

You may be questioning, "Why would God show us things to come?" Because we are part of the Abrahamic covenant. God was about to destroy a city that had a relative of Abraham in it, and because of Abraham's covenant with God, God said, "I'm going to tell him," and He did.

And Abraham came near and said, "Would you also destroy the righteous with the wicked?

"Suppose there were fifty righteous within the city; would You also destroy the place and not spare it for the fifty righteous that were in it?"

Genesis 18:23,24

Abraham went on until he got down to ten. He asked God, **"Suppose ten should be found there?"** God answered, **"I will not destroy it for the sake of ten"** (Genesis 18:32).

Not only will God show you things to come, but *you will have power in intercession*. If the fire of God falls on a city, you need to believe that because of your covenant with God, He will save your relatives. We have a New Testament family salvation promise in Acts 16:31: **"Believe on the Lord Jesus Christ, and you will be saved, you and your household."**

There is only one reason Lot escaped destruction and came out of Sodom before the fire fell: *Abraham, his relative, was in covenant with God*. God honored that relationship.

You may be questioning, "Will my relatives be saved?" As the seed of Abraham, stand on your covenant promises. (All of the promises in God's Word are "covenant promises" to the born-again believer.) Lot was removed seconds before the brimstone dropped out of the clouds!

If you are a believer in Jesus Christ, then you are Abraham's seed and an heir to the same promises that God made to Abraham. God prospered Abraham, protected him and revealed to him things to come. As a born-again believer, you are an heir to this same type of relationship.

In Genesis, chapter 22, God called Abraham to take his only son Isaac, a miracle child, and offer him as a sacrifice on Mount Moriah. Abraham went through the process, and when he raised the knife to slay his only son, an angel of the Lord stopped him and said:

"Do not lay your hand on the lad, or do anything to him; for now I know that you fear God, since you have not withheld your son, your only son, from Me."

Then Abraham lifted his eyes and looked, and there behind him was a ram caught in a thicket by its horns. So Abraham went and took the ram, and offered it up for a burnt offering instead of his son.

And Abraham called the name of the place, The-Lord-Will-Provide. [*The King James Version* calls it **"Jehovah-Jireh."**]

Genesis 22:12-14

Abraham had a second revelation of Who God is: "Not only is He El Shaddai, the God Who is more than enough, but He is *my* provider, Almighty God, the God Who has everything I need."

"...as it is said to this day, 'In the Mount of the Lord it shall be provided'" (Genesis 22:14). *Jehovah Jireh* means the God Who sees ahead and makes provision. The blessing of Abraham includes provision of everything you need. Part of the Abrahamic covenant is that God will provide. You may be thinking, "But I don't see it." Abraham didn't see it until he *completely obeyed God.*

God will even provide the offerings we want to bring to Him. A couple in our church was believing God for $1,000 to plant as a seed into our building fund. They didn't have it, so they planted a portion of it as a tithe toward it, then stood in faith believing God for the rest of it to come. The remainder of the $1,000 seed came supernaturally. You, too, can believe for seed to sow.

The other side of the Abrahamic covenant is: To get Abraham's blessings requires the Abraham kind of faith and obedience. The result of Abraham's obedience is shared in Genesis, chapter 22, verses 16-18:

> **"By Myself I have sworn, says the Lord, because you have done this thing, and have not withheld your son, your only son —**
>
> **"Blessing I will bless you, and multiplying I will multiply your descendants as the stars of the heaven and as the sand which is on the seashore; and your descendants shall possess the gate of their enemies.**
>
> **"In your seed all the nations of the earth shall be blessed, because you have obeyed My voice."**

At the end of his life, it was said of Abram, **"...the Lord had blessed Abraham in all things"** (Genesis 24:1). *Obedience* to the voice of the Lord, which came out of relationship, was a vital key to Abraham being so blessed. It is still a key to receiving the abundance God has planned for you!

Abundant Living Confessions

Here are ten Abundant Living Personalized Confessions from Chapter 3, which will help to move you into the mainstream of God's abundance:

1. As a born-again believer, I am an heir of the same promises God gave to Abraham.
2. I am blessed with Abraham's blessings so I can be a blessing to others.
3. God is the Source of everything that has been entrusted to me.
4. God is El Shaddai, the all-sufficient One, in my life.
5. God said to Abram, "I will multiply you exceedingly" (Genesis 17:2), and "I will make you exceedingly

27

fruitful" (v. 6). These are God's promises to me. He is multiplying me exceedingly and making me exceedingly fruitful.

6. I abide in the Lord and He abides in me. He has appointed and anointed me to bear fruit that will remain (John 15:5,16).

7. I was grafted into the covenant when I yielded to the lordship of Jesus Christ.

8. My old nature of sin has been replaced with a new nature of righteousness (2 Corinthians 5:21).

9. God is Jehovah Jireh to me — the God Who sees ahead and provides for my every need.

10. To get Abraham's blessings requires Abraham's kind of *faith* and *obedience*. I will believe God's Word, speak His Word, obey it, and expect to see a manifestation of it!

CHAPTER 4
IT'S TIME FOR
"LIFE MORE ABUNDANTLY"

Jesus identified the devil as a liar, a thief, a killer and a destroyer. That's the devil's complete job description — and it never changes. Jesus said of the devil, **"He was a murderer from the beginning, and does not stand in the truth, because there is no truth in him...he is a liar and the father of it"** (John 8:44). Jesus also said of him, **"The thief does not come except to steal, and to kill, and to destroy..."** (John 10:10).

In this same verse, Jesus describes His role in our lives: **"...I have come that they may have life, and that they may have it *more abundantly*."** In verse 11 Jesus continues to explain His role: **"I am the good shepherd. The good shepherd gives His life for the sheep."**

More abundantly means "more abundantly"! Another way of saying it is, "I want to give you life in all its fullness, until it overflows." God is a God of total abundance.

Think about the Milky Way. Think about the fish in the ocean, the birds of the air, the grass, the trees, the plants. Everything God does, He does it in *abundance* because that's His nature. He is a God of abundance, and because He is, He wants us to begin to think *abundance* in our lives. Why should we think lack or accept it when we have such an abundant God Who wants us to have life "more abundantly"?

Maybe you have said, "I just want a little peace." God wants to give you peace **"which surpasses all understanding"** (Philippians 4:7). Or, you've said, "I'd like to have a little fun." God wants to give you **"joy unspeakable and full of glory"** (1 Peter 1:8 KJV).

Jesus is our Jubilee, so we can experience the year of Jubilee each day of every year, which is *the year of God's favor*.

God's will is that we would experience abundant grace. Lamentations 3:22,23 KJV says, **"It is of the Lord's mercies that we are not consumed, because his compassions fail not. They are new every morning: great is thy faithfulness."**

You may feel like you exhausted God's grace before you were saved, but an overflow of His grace and mercy is available to you every day.

How To Tap Into God's Abundance

In Matthew 6:25-34 Jesus talks about His abundant provision and how we can tap into it:

"Therefore I say to you, do not worry about your life, what you will eat or what you will drink; nor about your body, what you will put on. Is not life more than food and the body more than clothing?

"Look at the birds of the air, for they neither sow nor reap nor gather into barns; yet your heavenly Father feeds them. Are you not of more value than they?

"Which of you by worrying can add one cubit to his stature?

"So why do you worry about clothing? Consider the lilies of the field, how they grow: they neither toil nor spin;

"And yet I say to you that even Solomon in all his glory was not arrayed like one of these.

"Now if God so clothes the grass of the field, which today is, and tomorrow is thrown into the oven, will He not much more clothe you, O you of little faith?

"Therefore do not worry, saying, 'What shall we eat?' or 'What shall we drink?' or 'What shall we wear?'

"For after all these things the Gentiles seek. For your heavenly Father knows that you need all these things.

"But seek first the kingdom of God and His righteousness, and all these things shall be added to you. [This is one of the primary keys to your prosperity.]

"Therefore do not worry about tomorrow, for tomorrow will worry about its own things. Sufficient for the day is its own trouble."

Replacing a Poverty Mentality
With the Knowledge of God's Goodness

There is a poverty and lack mentality in some people that is against the will and purpose of God. Jesus said, **"I have come that they may have life, and that they may have it more abundantly"** (John 10:10).

You may be praying, "Oh, Lord, I need some power in my life." Yet Romans 8:11 says, **"But if the Spirit of Him who raised Jesus from the dead dwells in you, He who raised Christ from the dead will also give life to your mortal bodies through His Spirit who dwells in you."** How much power do you need? Do you need more power than it took to raise Jesus from death, hell and the grave, to defeat the devil and destroy principalities and powers?

Much of our problem is halfway between our ears! It's in our thinking, because Ephesians 1:3 says God **"...has blessed us with every spiritual blessing in the heavenly places in Christ."**

Philippians 4:19 says, **"And my God shall supply all your need according to His riches in glory by Christ Jesus."** So is our supply dependent upon the U.S. Treasury? The world bank? No! Our Source is literally out of this world! We cannot be touched by the earth's inflation, by rust, or by thieves. Everything God has for us is incorruptible. Psalm 23 conveys the same thought to us: Jesus came that we might have life and have it more abundantly.

31

Your comprehension of God's love for you will directly affect your faith to believe for God's abundance. When you discovered that God loved you enough to give His Son, Jesus Christ, to die on the cross for you, to pay for your sins, to go through death, hell and be raised from the dead, then you had faith to believe that He could save you. Your faith was related to your understanding of how much God loves you and cares about you.

In John 3:16,17 Jesus said:

For God so loved the world that He gave His only begotten Son, that whoever believes in Him should not perish but have everlasting life.

For God did not send His Son into the world to condemn the world, but that the world through Him might be saved.

James got a revelation of how good God is. In chapter 1, verse 17, he says, **"Every good gift and every perfect gift is from above, and comes down from the Father of lights, with whom there is no variation or shadow of turning."**

Jesus is trying to help us gain an understanding that "good" comes from God and "evil" comes from the devil. In essence He is saying, "It's the thief (the devil) who is stealing from you. It's the devil who is killing and destroying. It is not Me, and neither is it My Father. I was not sent to condemn the world but to save it."

You may have needs right now and it's beyond your imagination that God could possibly meet them. But as you get a revelation of how much He loves you, faith will leap in your heart and abundance will come your way.

Some people have lived in depression for years because of a lack mentality. Others have been grouches, grumblers and complainers, but when they get a revelation that God is making them more than conquerors, no longer are they going to be worried, anxious and fearful.

Provision of the Good Shepherd

Psalm 23:1 says, **"The Lord is my shepherd; I shall not want."** In other words, "I shall not lack. I shall not do without." Jesus said, **"I am the good shepherd"** (John 10:11). In other words, "If I am your Shepherd, I am going to *increase* you, not steal from you."

This is the same thing Jesus was saying in Matthew 6:33: **"But seek first the kingdom of God and His righteousness, and all these things shall be added to you."** When you spend your life seeking the Kingdom of God, God will continually add to you everything that you need.

Some people know about "the" Shepherd, but David was declaring, "He is *my* Shepherd." It's important that you take this as a personal statement: "I have a Good Shepherd, and He wants life and life more abundantly for me."

> **He makes me to lie down in green pastures; He leads me beside the still waters.**
>
> **He restores my soul; He leads me in the paths of righteousness for His name's sake.**
>
> **Psalm 23:2,3**

Green pastures and water are the primary needs for sheep. If you have seen barren desert land — all dried up and parched, the grass gone, and starving animals trying to find something to eat, their bones sunken in — I think you can see how important it is to come into a green pasture. God wants to paint you a picture of lush, green pastures. He doesn't want you to be in a place of barrenness, but in a place of *productivity*, with *plenty of everything!* He wants you *totally blessed!*

It is *not* God's will that you live through a day without the joy of the Lord overflowing in your life. Paul said, **"I can do all things through Christ who strengthens me"** (Philippians 4:13). I want to change your thinking. Start believing for the strength of the Lord in your life.

Psalm 27:1 says, **"The Lord is my light and my salva-tion; whom shall I fear?** *The Lord is the strength of my life; of whom shall I be afraid?"* Some people have a "barely get by" mentality, whether it is in strength or finances. To them, God is always just barely enough. It's time to change your think-ing. He is the God Who is more than enough!

Jesus said to two blind men who cried out to Him for mercy, **"According to** *your faith* **let it be to you"** (Matthew 9:29). Their eyes were opened. Jesus said to the woman with the issue of blood, **"Daughter,** *your faith* **has made you well. Go in peace, and be healed of your affliction"** (Mark 5:34).

Life will begin to change for you if you begin to believe in a God Who is a God of abundance, and believe in a Savior Who wants to do exceeding abundantly above all that you could ever ask, hope, dream, think, or desire. Live with that expectation and praise God for it.

When Sharon and I began preaching in Tulsa, we had approximately 300 people on Sunday morning and 25 people on Wednesday nights. God showed us in a vision the growth that would come. It happened and it is still happening. We doubled to 600 people in a very short time. Then we doubled again to 1,200 people. Today we have more than 10,000 people in our congregation and we're still growing. God is the God of abundance.

Do you have a "cut off" point to stop God's blessings from coming to you? "Just bless me this much, Lord, then stop. I think I'll bankrupt heaven if You give me any more." That's the way a lot of people think. Why not just believe for all God has for you, then share it with all those who are around you? If you get an overflow of joy, pass it on. If you get an extra load of peace, share it. Begin to believe for God's abundance in every area. God is calling us to live in the overflow!

Psalm 23:4 says, **"Yea, though I walk through the valley of the shadow of death, I will fear no evil...."** If you serve the

God of abundance, then you are not believing for evil to come to your life, but you are believing for divine protection. I think one of the greatest areas to get a revelation of God's abundance is in freedom from cares, worries, anxieties and fears. They are robbers. It is not abundant life to be fretting, fuming, worrying and harassed and tormented over what is going on in your life.

How can we live without fear? By knowing that God is with us. Jehovah Jireh, your provider, is with you; Jehovah Rapha, your healer, is with you; Jehovah Nissi, your banner and victory, is with you; Jehovah M'Kaddesh, your sanctifier, is with you; Jehovah Shalom, your peace, is with you; Jehovah Rohi, your shepherd and protector, is with you; Jehovah Tsidkenu, your redemption and righteousness, is with you. Jehovah Shammah, your ever-present Friend, is with you. Why should you fear any situation? People fear when they forget Who God is.

Psalm 23 is a personalized confession of faith and a confession of the blessing of a relationship with God. People from all denominations from all over the world love this psalm.

"...For you are with me; Your rod and Your staff [your Word and your Spirit], **they comfort me"** (Psalm 23:4). God's Word and His Spirit guide, guard and protect, just like a rod and a staff in the hands of a shepherd watching over his flock.

"You prepare a table before me in the presence of my enemies..." (v. 5). This is talking about here on the earth now, because in heaven we won't have any enemies. In a world filled with devils, we're going to have a table of abundance spread before us!

You may be saying, "It hasn't happened to me." That's why I am sharing this word with you, to move you from your circumstances and your belief system of a table of emptiness and a mentality of lack, to a table of abundance and to a revelation of a God of abundance. Until your thinking changes, your circumstances won't change. *How you perceive God's blessings and provision will determine what you believe and what you receive.*

With your heart you can be trying your very best to serve God, but if your thinking is wrong, it will mess up your believing. This is why the Bible says we are transformed by the renewing of our mind. We must renew our thinking to be in agreement with God's will and purposes (Romans 12:2).

"...You anoint my head with oil..." (v. 5). If you have been praying for a fresh anointing, why not start by confessing Psalm 23:5? Each day declare, "Thank You, Lord, for anointing me with fresh oil." You don't have to be in a special meeting or around special people, because you have a relationship with the most special Person of all, Jesus Christ. Thank God for people and for services where you can be ministered to, but I want to encourage you, God's Word works in the middle of the night. When you're all alone and no one else is around, you can speak God's Word.

"...my cup runs over" (v. 5). See yourself with an overflowing cup. Some people's thinking has been, "I'll believe it when I see it." We are moving out of being ruled by circumstances, dominated by our feelings, and controlled by our senses into the realm where *we walk by faith and not by sight.* We take God's Word over the word of the world, over the opinions of others and over our feelings or circumstances, and we begin to speak it: "God is causing my cup to run over. His abundance is filling my life."

You have to believe in God's provision, act as if you already have it and get your mouth talking like it. Then you will begin to see it. Faith always carries the load. It's like the engine of a train. Many people try to run their train with their caboose — their feelings. That's why they are not going anywhere. They are parked on the tracks. You have to hook up to the engine of faith and start making your feelings go the direction your faith is going.

"Surely goodness and mercy shall follow me all the days of my life..." (v. 6). Your comprehension of God's love for you will set the level of your faith to release God's abundance into your life. Some people look back to when they were a sinner, far from God. They have the concept that they are too far gone, they have done too much, they are too bad. Then one day they find out how much God loves them, and He reaches down and saves them. What would happen if you got a revelation of God's love for you?

As we began pastoring, the vision for growth began to come. The church started in a car dealership with ten acres of land. In my mind, I could not see beyond that car dealership. It was a wonderful expansion for us — three times the amount of acreage we had at the previous site.

One day as I was explaining to one of our board members how we were going to build another story on to this car dealership, he just looked at me and said, "Billy Joe, you need fifty acres or more. I see a big expanse of land that God is going to give this church." I was going, "You do?" At that time my mind could not comprehend it. It was exceeding abundantly above all I could ask or think. Today we have more land than we dreamed about.

God has some things for you that may be out of your mind right now. They are down in your spirit, so you've got to work on taking an elevator and going all the way to the top!

Getting a Revelation of God's Love for You

Ephesians, chapter 3, contains a prayer for strengthening your inner man. The revelation of the love of God is going to come to you through your inner man. That's why the baptism of the Holy Spirit (the power of the Spirit) is so awesome. It enables us to tap into things inside of our spirit and get them up into our mind through interpretation and revelation by the Holy Spirit. He's saying, "I'm praying you will be strengthened so that you can know the love of Christ."

37

>   **For this reason I bow my knees to the Father of our Lord Jesus Christ,**
>
>   **From whom the whole family in heaven and earth is named,**
>
>   **That He would grant you, according to the riches of His glory, to be strengthened with might through His Spirit in the inner man,**
>
>   **That Christ may dwell in your hearts through faith; that you, being rooted and grounded in love,**
>
>   **May be able to comprehend with all the saints what is the width and length and depth and height —**
>
>   **To know the love of Christ....**
>
>   **Ephesians 3:14-19**

Do you know how much God loves you and how much He has planned for your life? People ask me, "Did you have in your mind the things that would happen to you?" We had little flashes, but what God is doing is so far beyond our thinking. Even now, we sense we've only scratched the surface. We think God has great things for *all believers*.

Verse 19 of Ephesians, chapter 3, says: **"To know the love of Christ which passes knowledge; that you may be filled with all the fullness of God."** How are we filled with the fullness of God? When we get a revelation of God's love for us and we open our heart up to accept, "The Lord is my shepherd. I am not going to be afraid today. I am not going to live with worry and fear. I am going to let You live in me in all Your fullness today, Lord — all Your peace, Your joy, Your victory."

But it doesn't stop there. Verse 20 says, **"Now to Him who is able to do exceedingly abundantly above all that we ask or think, according to the power that works in us."** We're back to the idea of our cup overflowing, life and life more abundantly. We're back into that place where a little boy shares his sack lunch of five loaves and two fish, and 5,000 men, plus women and children, are fed. Then the little boy goes home with twelve baskets full, after everyone is fed (Matthew 14:17-21).

Do we serve a God Who is more than enough? What does He want you to take home with you? We've had a mentality like the disciples, "Lord, there is not enough money to feed all these people. It's too far, too late and too little." Their thinking had to be changed.

Have you ever thought about why Jesus said to Peter after he had fished all night and caught nothing, **"Launch out into the deep and let down your nets for a catch"** (Luke 5:4)? Simon Peter answered Jesus, **"Master, we have toiled all night and caught nothing; nevertheless at Your word I will let down the net"** (v. 5).

Verse 6 says, **"And when they had done this, they caught a great number of fish, and their net was breaking."** The catch was so great their boats began to sink. Jesus said to Peter, **"Do not be afraid. From now on you will catch men"** (v. 10).

Jesus was trying to explode Peter's thinking by giving him a picture of an overflow. Little did Peter know that about three years later he would be preaching on the Day of Pentecost and 3,000 people would come out of the devil's kingdom and move into God's Kingdom — a net-breaking, boat-sinking load! He was just a fisherman, but God saw the potential in him like He sees in you and me. I'm telling you, God is able to do exceeding abundantly above all you can ask, hope, think, dream, or desire in every area of your life.

It's time to quit talking about how little you grew up with and realize, "I'm in a new family. I've got a new Father, a new bloodline. I've got a bank account in heaven, and I'm drawing on it."

Abundant Living Confessions

Here are sixteen Abundant Living Personalized Confessions from Chapter 4, which will help to move you into the mainstream of God's abundance:

1. Jesus is my Good Shepherd, the One Who has provided abundant, overflowing life for me.
2. As I seek first the Kingdom of God and His righteousness, everything I need God will add unto me (Matthew 6:33).
3. The same Spirit that raised Jesus from the dead dwells in me (Romans 8:11).
4. God has blessed me with every spiritual blessing (Ephesians 1:3).
5. God supplies *all* of my need according to His riches in glory by Christ Jesus (Philippians 4:19).
6. God loves me unconditionally. He came to lift me, not to condemn me (John 3:16,17).
7. Every good and perfect gift comes from God (James 1:17).
8. Because Jesus is my Shepherd, I shall not want (Psalm 23:1).
9. God wants me in a place of productivity, with plenty of everything.
10. I can do all things through Christ Who strengthens me (Philippians 4:13).
11. The Lord is the strength of my life (Psalm 27:1).
12. Jehovah Jireh, my provider, is with me. Jehovah Rapha, my healer, is with me. Jehovah Nissi, my banner and victory, is with me. Jehovah M'Kaddesh, my sanctifier, is with me. Jehovah Shalom, my peace, is with me. Jehovah Rohi, my shepherd and protector, is with me. Jehovah Tsidkenu, my redemption and righteousness, is with me. Jehovah Shammah, my ever-present Friend, is with me.
13. God's Word and His Spirit guide, guard, comfort and protect me (Psalm 23:4).
14. God has prepared a table of abundance for me in the presence of my enemies (Psalm 23:5).

15. God's goodness and mercy follow me every day of my life (Psalm 23:6).
16. God is able to do "exceedingly abundantly" above all that I have asked or thought because of the Holy Ghost power that is at work in me (Ephesians 3:20).

CHAPTER 5

Seedtime and Harvest —
God's Avenue of Increase

**While the earth remains, *seedtime and harvest*, cold
and heat, winter and summer, and day and night shall
not cease.**

Genesis 8:22

God put certain laws in the universe that operate for our
benefit. One such law is that of seedtime and harvest,
or what I will also refer to as the laws of divine prosperity, sowing and reaping, or giving and receiving.

We could say it another way. It is the law of receiving God's
abundance so you can give with all liberality to your local church
and then to those in need of food, clothing and shelter, and to
support the spreading of the Gospel to all nations.

You can sow to receive the things you need, desire and
believe God wants you to have in this life. The seedtime and
harvest principle is a way of life.

The provision for seedtime is found in the harvest, and the
provision for the harvest is found in the seedtime. There is a
cycle where one provides for the other. Out of the harvest comes
the seed, and out of the seedtime comes the harvest.

You can apply the laws of seedtime and harvest to every
facet of your life, because the Bible says, **"...Whatever a man
sows, that he will also reap"** (Galatians 6:7).

Your heart is like a field. When you sow the incorruptible
seed of God's Word into your heart, it will produce in your life.
This is why God said to Joshua:

43

> **This Book of the Law shall not depart from your mouth, but you shall meditate in it day and night, that you may observe to do according to all that is written in it. For then you will make your way prosperous, and then you will have good success.**
>
> **Joshua 1:8**

As you plant the seed of the Word in your life by believing it and speaking it aloud, you can expect a harvest. You are responsible for the sowing, watering, fertilizing, protecting and taking the oversight of the seed of the Word that you sow.

A unique principle about seed is that it multiplies itself. It's not an addition principle, but a multiplication principle that if you sow one seed of corn, one stalk may have two or three ears on it. Each ear might have 3,000 kernels of corn on it. With one seed, you have not added but you have multiplied your seed.

Some people need friends. Perhaps you have said, "I wish people would be friendlier to me." Showing friendliness and ministering kindness can be seeds that, if sown in faith, will reap a harvest of friendship and kindness. I expect people to love and respect me. I expect even my enemies to be at peace with me, because Proverbs 16:7 says, **"When a man's ways please the Lord, He makes even his enemies to be at peace with him."**

After my father passed away, the Spirit of God dealt with me to talk to my mom about how to come out of the tremendous shock of losing the closest person in her life. I said, "Mom, you need to go to the hospitals and nursing homes and visit the sick and visit some of the other ladies in the church who are alone." Because she gave love, time and effort to others, depression and grief never came on her.

Many people get caught in a situation where they want to reap a harvest, but they haven't sown any seed. You may say, "I want someone to love me and care for me." If you are continually sowing that kind of seed, you won't lack for a harvest of love and care.

The seed contains within itself the power to reproduce itself in fruit, and that fruit contains within itself the seed to plant for more fruit. Sometimes people only go one cycle. They plant and when they reap the fruit, they eat all of it.

When you reap, you should remember that in that harvest there is food to eat and more seed to sow, whether it's time, love, concern, financial, spiritual, material blessings, or whatever it might be. Don't eat all of your seed!

Believers are catching hold of the principle of "seedtime and harvest" and are sowing by faith. Though they have begun with only a small proportion of the world's resources, the wealth of the world is now beginning to flow into the Body of Christ. As we continue to sow, we will take possession of more and more of the wealth of the wicked.

The same principle applies to the spiritual arena. Some people who have had experiences with God, the knowledge of God and the Word of God have said, "We've got all there is, and we know all there is to know. We don't need to seek God anymore. We don't need to be open to the Holy Spirit to reveal new things to us, because we are satisfied where we are." The sad truth is, they stay right where they are.

On the other hand, there is a group of people who have said, "We want all of God there is. We want the Holy Spirit. We want the revelation of healing and deliverance. We want the Word of God in all of its fullness." They have been sowing time in the Word, listening to tapes, reading books and going to services several times a week. All they talk about is Jesus. They will increase!

For too long people have looked negatively at the laws of seedtime and harvest. God didn't put these laws in the earth so we could sow something bad and reap something bad. However, because it is a spiritual law or principle, if you sow bad seed, you will reap a bad harvest.

45

Similarly, God didn't put gravity in the earth so people could jump off buildings. Gravity will work negatively if you do the wrong thing in relationship to it. God put gravity in the earth because it is one of His laws that keeps the universe going in the right way.

It is the same way with the laws of seedtime and harvest. God put these laws in the earth to keep the earth going, to keep His Word going and to keep us going. By understanding the laws of seedtime and harvest, we can apply this principle to every area of life. With these laws, our needs are connected with God's supply.

Here are five facts to help you better understand how the laws of seedtime and harvest work:

1. *Seedtime always precedes the harvest.*

To receive a harvest in your life, you must plant seed. Oral Roberts gave a very simple illustration of the laws of seedtime and harvest. He said that it wouldn't be right to go to a coke machine and reach down where the coke comes out and try to get a coke if you didn't put any money in the machine. But if you put your money in, then you have every right to expect a coke to come out of that machine.

It's the same way with seedtime and harvest. You don't have a right to expect a harvest until you have planted seed.

2. *When you plant seed, expect a harvest.*

When a farmer plants seed, he expects a harvest. No farmer has ever said, "I think I'll just plant some corn seed this year and forget about the harvest." He expects a return on that which he has planted. Likewise, you should expect a harvest on the seed you plant.

3. *Seed multiplies.*

Seed doesn't just add to itself, but it is multiplied back in return. If a person plants one seed, he is not going to end up with just two seeds at the end of the year. If it is planted and all the conditions are met, he will receive a multiplied number of seeds: thirty-, sixty-, or a hundredfold.

The laws of seedtime and harvest say, "If you have a lack in your life, you can sow toward replacing that lack with bounty."

If you have a need to grow spiritually, you can sow time in the Word and in prayer and receive the spiritual blessings which you desire.

When I first saw people who were operating in the realm of faith and the great things that were happening to them, I thought I could never have those kinds of experiences. Then the Spirit of God began to show me, "If you will sow the same kind of seed they have sown, you will get the same results." They're not getting it because they are special. They are getting it because the seedtime and harvest principle works. If the Word is planted, it will produce.

4.   *A seed has the ability to reproduce itself in exact likeness and kind.*

Then God said, "Let the earth bring forth grass, the herb that yields seed, and the fruit tree that yields fruit according to its kind, whose seed is in itself, on the earth"; and it was so.

And the earth brought forth grass, the herb that yields seed according to its kind, and the tree that yields fruit, whose seed is in itself according to its kind. And God saw that it was good.

Genesis 1:11,12

If you plant an apple seed, you will get apples. The seeds inside of it will be an exact likeness of the first seed that was planted. If you plant apple seeds, inside of that apple you won't find watermelon seeds! The seeds will look like the very same seeds that were planted.

5.   *Within every harvest will be the seed for your next planting.*

Within the harvest is provision for eating as well as provision for your next planting. There is a revolving cycle that out

47

of every harvest, there will be provision for you and more seed to sow.

Galatians 6:7 says, **"Do not be deceived, God is not mocked; for whatever a man sows, that he will also reap."** *Whatever* implies that we are dealing with more than finances.

We have seen this principle work with our children. The way we treat them is the way they treat other people. If you want a certain trait or fruit to come out of your children, you can sow into their lives and it will come back.

As a businessman or woman, you can sow honesty and reap the rewards of honesty. You can sow generosity or kindness and it will come back to you. If you sow gentleness, you will reap gentleness. Although these things aren't tangible, they will bring a return. Both the tangible and the intangible will produce a harvest.

Several years ago when Sharon and I went home to visit our parents for the holidays, we went to see a man who had started a men's suit shop a few years earlier. He didn't know a thing about suits, and he hardly knew how to match his socks. But God dealt with him to start a men's suit shop.

He said, "It was hilarious the first time I went to market. I didn't know what to order, so I just started picking out things. Everything sold that I selected." He began in a very small shop, but it became the largest suit store in all of southwest Arkansas.

People came from all over that part of the country to shop in his store. I watched him, because if a person is doing that kind of business, I want to know the principles in which he is operating.

When people walked into his store, he greeted them and got acquainted with them. The clerks did the same thing. They weren't just selling clothes. They ministered love and kindness to the people. Even the people who didn't know Jesus received His love through these business people. They gave good deals on suits and excellent service. Finally, the owner was a tither.

By sowing the right seeds he received a good harvest. When a need is met in your life, you will go back to where it was met. Your body will lead you there because of the atmosphere. With any work, business or ministry the laws are the same.

There will be a return in like kind to that which you are sowing. When you sow blessing, you will reap blessing. When you sow favor, you will reap favor. You can confess all the Scriptures you want about having favor, but if you don't sow favor, you'll not receive it in the dimension you desire.

It's time to take inventory of what you have been sowing and what you are reaping. In Christ, *you* have the power to change what you are sowing and what you are reaping.

Abundant Living Confessions

Here are ten Abundant Living Personalized Confessions from Chapter 5, which will help to move you into the mainstream of God's abundance:

1. God initiated the spiritual principle of seedtime and harvest as the basis for my prosperity (Genesis 8:22).
2. The primary purpose for being prospered God's way is to support the propagation of the Gospel of Jesus Christ throughout the earth.
3. The seedtime and harvest principle is a way of life, and it applies to every facet of my life.
4. Whatever I sow, I will reap in like kind (Galatians 6:7).
5. To meditate in God's Word day and night and then walk in obedience to it, is God's guideline to me for achieving divine prosperity and success (Joshua 1:8).
6. Within every harvest is my seed for planting a new crop, whether it is kindness, love, respect, finances, honesty, generosity, or gentleness.
7. As I obey God's laws of seedtime and harvest, the wealth of the world will be loosed into my hands.

8. If I sow good seed, I will reap a good harvest; but if I sow bad seed, I will reap a bad harvest. Everything I sow reproduces in like kind.

9. As I obey God's laws of divine prosperity, my needs are connected with God's supply.

10. As I sow time in the Word and in prayer, I will reap a harvest of spiritual blessings.

CHAPTER 6
GIVING WITH EXPECTANCY

When I was growing up, I cannot remember hearing a message about God wanting us to have abundance. We believed in the great things that Jesus had done and the wonderful stories in the Bible, but the concept of God's abundance in the earth being something for me or for another individual never crossed my mind. Only after I was born again and Spirit filled did I begin to hear that God created the earth and everything in it with humanity in mind.

God is not a distant idea, a philosophy in a book, or a set of commandments on a wall. He is a loving heavenly Father Who cares about your life. When people needed food, Jesus multiplied the loaves and fishes. When they needed healing, He healed them. When they needed deliverance from demonic oppression, Jesus delivered them. Whatever the need, He had more than enough to meet it. God has not changed. **"Jesus Christ is the same yesterday, today, and forever"** (Hebrews 13:8). He is still the God of abundance.

When you walk in obedience to God's will, your path is going to intersect His total provision of everything that you need.

The first step of tapping into God's abundance is to *believe God wants you blessed.*

Secondly, the goal of tapping into God's abundance is *relationship* with Him — walking and talking with Him, living with Him, obeying Him, serving Him and loving Him all the days of your life.

Thirdly, the focus of your life must be the Person of Jesus. Matthew 6:33 actually means, *we want to be right with God, full of His peace, walking in His joy. We want to have God's Kingdom ruling on the inside of us with Jesus as Lord, directing our lives in what we are doing on a daily basis.* That's what it means to seek first the Kingdom of God and His righteousness. He's calling the shots and we are listening to Him. He is directing us through His written Word and through the Holy Spirit's guidance as we daily commune with Him in prayer.

Let's put it in a practical way. If you don't love your brother, your neighbor, or your fellow employee, you can be doing a lot of things concerning how to obtain prosperity and blessing, but it will not work. If on the one hand you're attempting to achieve increase, blessing and abundance, but on the other hand you are operating outside of the love of God in bitterness, resentment and unforgiveness, it won't work. Faith works by love (Galatians 5:6).

If you're operating in gluttony, gossip, slander, backbiting, unholiness and impurity, you are blocking the release of God's blessings in your life. And if we are going to live in God's abundance, we are going to have to live in His holiness.

Ask yourself, "Am I meeting God's conditions of seeking His Kingdom first? Do I give God the first hour of every day that I live?" How can you expect to prosper if the first and best part of your day is given to something other than God?

Do you give the first day of every week to God in worship and service? Many people no longer regard any day as holy. All of them are secular and there is no day set aside to worship and honor the Lord. On the seventh day God rested. Jesus was raised on what we call the first day of the week, Sunday morning.

Do you give God the first dollar out of every ten that you earn? Do you give Him your best in worship and praise? Is your prayer life consistent? Are you watching TV programs and/or videos or listening to music that is contrary to God's Kingdom principles?

You see, if we don't seek God's Kingdom first in these areas, He is not going to add to us the things that we need. He said if we would put His Kingdom first, everything we need would be added to us.

The rich young ruler who came to Jesus had lots of money, but he didn't have Jesus ruling his life. Let's pick up on this account in Mark, chapter 10.

The rich young ruler asked Jesus:

> **"Good Teacher, what shall I do that I may inherit eternal life?"**
>
> **Verse 17**

Jesus answered:

> **"Why do you call Me good? No one is good but One, that is, God.**
>
> **"You know the commandments: 'Do not commit adultery,' 'Do not murder,' 'Do not steal,' 'Do not bear false witness,' 'Do not defraud,' 'Honor your father and your mother.' "**
>
> **Verses 18,19**

The rich young ruler answered, **"Teacher, all these things I have kept from my youth"** (v. 20). Jesus said, **"One thing you lack: Go your way, sell whatever you have and give to the poor, and you will have treasure in heaven; and come, take up the cross, and follow Me"** (v. 21).

This young man lacked one thing: *He did not put God first.* He held on to his possessions and rejected the Lord's directive.

For some people, their first love and primary focus is on sports. For this young man it was money. For some people it's clothes or their job. The young man walked away grieved. Jesus said to His disciples, **"How hard it is for those who have riches to enter the kingdom of God!"** (v. 23). Jesus repeated a second time, **"Children, how hard it is for those who *trust in riches* to enter the kingdom of God!"** (v. 24). This is consistent with what we read in Matthew, chapter 6.

Scripture says the disciples were astonished at Jesus' words to the rich young ruler, so they asked Him, **"Who then can be saved?"** (v. 26). Jesus said, **"With men it is impossible, but not with God; for with God all things are possible"** (v. 27). Peter said, **"See, we have left all and followed You"** (v. 28). Here is Jesus' response:

> **"Assuredly, I say to you, there is no one who has left house or brothers or sisters or father or mother or wife or children or lands, for My sake and the gospel's,**
>
> **"Who shall not receive a hundredfold now in this time — houses and brothers and sisters and mothers and children and lands, with persecutions — and in the age to come, eternal life."**
>
> **Mark 10:29,30**

There will be persecution for anyone who goes after the Kingdom of God with all their being. Jesus very clearly separated when we leave this planet (eternal life) from before we leave. He spoke of the *hundredfold return harvest* in this life.

Another key to living in God's abundance is *give as an act of your faith*. Your giving sets a standard for your receiving. Limited giving means limited receiving. Just as a farmer decides the harvest he wants by the seed that he plants, so we decide our harvest by what we give.

Paul admonishes us in our giving in 2 Corinthians 9:6-11:

> **But this I say: He who sows sparingly will also reap sparingly, and he who sows bountifully will also reap bountifully.**
>
> **So let each one give as he purposes in his heart, not grudgingly or of necessity; for God loves a cheerful giver.**
>
> **And God is able to make all grace abound toward you, that you, always having all sufficiency in all things, may have an abundance for every good work.**
>
> **As it is written: "He has dispersed abroad, He has given to the poor; His righteousness endures forever."**
>
> **Now may He who supplies seed to the sower, and**

bread for food, supply and multiply the seed you have sown and increase the fruits of your righteousness,
   While you are enriched in everything for all liberality, which causes thanksgiving through us to God.

Verse 10 gives us four things God will do:

1.   Supply seed to the sower;
2.   Give bread for food;
3.   Supply and multiply the seed you have sown; and
4.   Increase the fruits of your righteousness (love, joy, peace, longsuffering, kindness, goodness, faithfulness, gentleness and self-control).

You may be deep in debt with lack and poverty all around you. What should you do?

1.   Believe that God is a God of abundance.
2.   Seek God's Kingdom first. (Live a life of holiness.)
3.   Determine to be a giver.

Let God be involved in every area of your life. It's a new day in the corporate world where people are realizing that it's okay to take God as their partner and invite the Holy Spirit in Monday through Friday during work hours as well as in their "off" hours.

People have tried to separate the sacred from the secular, and they only get the blessing on that area where they let God in. Let Him in every area, and He will cause all the things you plant to begin to multiply.

How would you like to be in a position where you could be a bountiful supplier of every good work so that every day you are causing people around the world to thank God? With God's help you can be in a position to bless missionaries, churches, Bible schools, medical works and feeding programs all over the earth and people will give thanks to God because of the bountiful harvest in your life.

We have people in our church who began to catch a vision of being a blessing to the world, and they have dedicated their businesses to God. Two of these families pay for our inspirational spots on two local network TV stations. Thousands of people each week hear the Gospel because of their generosity.

My challenge to you is to not only enter into giving, but start believing that you will receive so you can be a blessing. It will be unto you *according to your faith.* I believe many people have planted seeds, and because they didn't exercise their faith when they gave, they have dormant seed in the ground. Activate your faith by saying, "Lord, I believe those seeds are going to come up." Then water your seeds with the Word and with prayer.

When you get into the rhythm of believing in God as the God of abundance and break off a poverty mentality and a lack attitude, your harvest will begin to come and seed planting will increase. There are people who will be able to move into giving 30, 40, or even 50 percent of their income into the work of the Lord.

You may be questioning, "Why has this message of prosperity come at this hour in history?" Because this is the hour when we have the greatest opportunity in the world to take money and make it serve Jesus Christ rather than consume it upon our own lusts or hoard it. There are more people on earth who need Jesus than anytime in history.

Lay your financial affairs at the feet of Jesus and make a commitment: "Lord, I want every dime to touch a destiny, every nickel to have a name on it and every penny to represent a person, in Jesus' name."

Give with expectancy and your prosperity will increase continually.

Abundant Living Confessions

Here are nine Abundant Living Personalized Confessions from Chapter 6, which will help to move you into the mainstream of God's abundance:

1. God is a loving heavenly Father, and He cares about me.
2. My obedience to God will intersect His provision for everything that I need.
3. *Relationship* with Jesus is at the heart of living in God's abundance.
4. God directs my life through His written Word and through the counsel of the Holy Spirit.
5. Faith works by love (Galatians 5:6). I am learning more about the God-kind of love which suffers long and is kind. It does not envy or parade itself, it is not puffed up with pride, and it is not rude. It does not seek its own, is not easily provoked, thinks no evil, does not rejoice in iniquity but rejoices in truth. It bears all things, believes all things, hopes all things and endures all things. The God-kind of love is maturing in me. It never fails! (1 Corinthians 13:4-8).
6. To live in the fullness of God's abundance, I must live in His holiness.
7. My primary focus must be on the Lord and remain on the Lord, rather than on His blessings.
8. The hundredfold harvest is for me in this hour.
9. Abundant giving means abundant living. Limited giving means I will receive a limited return.

CHAPTER 7

How Much Should I Give?

> "Bring all the tithes into the storehouse, that there may be food in My house, and try Me now in this," says the Lord of hosts, "if I will not open for you the windows of heaven and pour out for you such blessing that there will not be room enough to receive it.
>
> "And I will rebuke the devourer for your sakes, so that he will not destroy the fruit of your ground, nor shall the vine fail to bear fruit for you in the field," says the Lord of hosts;
>
> "And all nations will call you blessed, for you will be a delightful land," says the Lord of hosts.
>
> Malachi 3:10-12

When you give as unto the Lord, it opens you up to receive the blessings of God. It will never diminish you, but it is God's avenue of increase.

There are people who have said, "I can't afford to tithe." I'll give you one better! You can't afford not to tithe, not when you understand the benefits of tithing which are spelled out in God's Word.

As you give of your tithes and offerings, you should expect the windows of heaven to be opened. You must believe that God will reward you according to the guidelines of His Word.

In verse 10 of Malachi, chapter 3, God says, "Try Me." *The King James Version* says, "Prove me." That means, "Put me to the test. I will rebuke the devourer for your sake."

Perhaps you have become a tither, yet you have had things that are contrary to the Word come against your life. The affliction and persecution have come to try to steal the Word out of your heart. Don't let go of God's promises just because you have not seen the total harvest of what the Word of God says. Remember, God cannot lie (Numbers 23:19), and His Word says, **"And let us not grow weary while doing good, for in due season we shall reap if we do not lose heart"** (Galatians 6:9).

Some people have said, "I have been tithing, and it seems like one calamity happens after another." Their words give life to the negatives that are happening. Put agreement with God's Word, and you will give life to His Word.

You need to settle it in your heart that God wants you to prosper. **"Beloved, I pray that you may prosper in all things and be in health, just as your soul prospers"** (3 John 2). Tithing is God's avenue for His prosperity to come to you. He wants you to prosper and live in abundance so you can be a blessing to others.

It is in giving of your tithes and offerings that fruit will abound to your account. Paul spoke of fruit abounding to the account of the Philippians because of their generosity in giving to him:

Nevertheless you have done well that you have shared in my distress.

Now you Philippians know also that in the beginning of the gospel, when I departed from Macedonia, no church shared with me concerning giving and receiving but you only.

For even in Thessalonica you sent aid once and again for my necessities.

Not that I seek the gift, but *I seek fruit that abounds to your account.*

Indeed I have all and abound. I am full, having received from Epaphroditus the things which were sent from you, a sweetsmelling aroma, an acceptable sacrifice, well pleasing to God.

> **And my God shall supply all your need according to His riches in glory by Christ Jesus.**
>
> **Philippians 4:14-19**

Paul was saying, "I am not concerned whether it looks like I have a lot or a little. God is my sufficiency. I live independent of circumstances. I can do all things through Christ Who strengthens me."

Paul indicated his love and concern for the Philippians when he said, **"Not that I seek the gift, but I seek the fruit that abounds to your account"** (v. 17).

As you get into the flow of giving and receiving, God's abundant provision will be released into your life.

Almsgiving

The giving of alms is giving to meet the needs of the poor. Caring for the poor is part of a true fast that the Spirit of God describes through the prophet Isaiah. He also gives some of the rewards of giving to those in need. Let's look at this account in Isaiah 58:6-14:

> **Is this not the fast that I have chosen: to loose the bonds of wickedness, to undo the heavy burdens, to let the oppressed go free, and that you break every yoke?**
>
> **Is it not to share your bread with the hungry, and that you bring to your house the poor who are cast out; when you see the naked, that you cover him, and not hide yourself from your own flesh?**
>
> **Then your light shall break forth like the morning, your healing shall spring forth speedily, and your righteousness shall go before you; the glory of the Lord shall be your rear guard.**
>
> **Then you shall call, and the Lord will answer; you shall cry, and He will say, "Here I am." If you take away the yoke from your midst, the pointing of the finger, and speaking wickedness,**
>
> **If you extend your soul to the hungry and satisfy the**

afflicted soul, then your light shall dawn in the darkness, and your darkness shall be as the noonday.

The Lord will guide you continually, and satisfy your soul in drought, and strengthen your bones; you shall be like a watered garden, and like a spring of water, whose waters do not fail.

Those from among you shall build the old waste places; you shall raise up the foundations of many generations; and you shall be called the Repairer of the Breach, the Restorer of Streets to Dwell In.

If you turn away your foot from the Sabbath, from doing your pleasure on My holy day, and call the Sabbath a delight, the holy day of the Lord honorable, and shall honor Him, not doing your own ways, not finding your own pleasure, nor speaking your own words,

Then you shall delight yourself in the Lord; and I will cause you to ride on the high hills of the earth, and feed you with the heritage of Jacob your father. The mouth of the Lord has spoken.

Psalm 41:1-3 lists the rewards of giving to meet the needs of the poor:

Blessed is he who considers the poor; the Lord will deliver him in time of trouble.

The Lord will preserve him and keep him alive, and he will be blessed on the earth; you will not deliver him to the will of his enemies.

The Lord will strengthen him on his bed of illness; you will sustain him on his sickbed.

Almsgiving — meeting the needs of the poor — is the work of every ministry that represents the Lord Jesus Christ. Obviously, the Church includes all believers in Jesus Christ, so individually and corporately, we are to be about the Father's business, and that includes meeting the needs of the poor.

God Will Be No Man's Debtor

In Luke, chapter 5, the multitudes crowded around Jesus to hear Him teach the Word of God. Because of the masses of people, Jesus got into Peter's boat, rowed out a short distance from shore and taught from the boat. When He was done teaching, He said to Peter, as a reward for allowing Him to use his boat, **"Launch out into the deep and let down your nets for a catch"** (Luke 5:4).

Let's look at the rest of the story which tells of Peter's reward for allowing Jesus to use his boat:

And when they had done this, they caught a great number of fish, and their net was breaking.

So they signaled to their partners in the other boat to come and help them. And they came and filled both the boats, so that they began to sink.

When Simon Peter saw it, he fell down at Jesus' knees, saying, "Depart from me, for I am a sinful man, O Lord!"

For he and all who were with him were astonished at the catch of fish which they had taken;

And so also were James and John, the sons of Zebedee, who were partners with Simon. And Jesus said to Simon, "Do not be afraid. From now on you will catch men."

So when they had brought their boats to land, they forsook all and followed Him.

Luke 5:6-11

This sounds like the windows of heaven were opened upon Peter. It sounds just like what God did for the Shunammite woman, who gave of what she had to Elisha, the prophet of God. Recognizing that Elisha was a holy man of God, she ministered to him as unto the Lord.

Now it happened one day that Elisha went to Shunem, where there was a notable woman, and she persuaded him to eat some food. So it was, as often as he passed by, that he would turn in there to eat some food.

And she said to her husband, "Look now, I know that this is a holy man of God, who passes by us regularly.

"Please, let us make a small upper room on the wall; and let us put a bed for him there, and a table and a chair and a lampstand; so it will be, whenever he comes to us, he can turn in there."

And it happened one day that he came there, and he turned in to the upper room and lay down there.

Then he said to Gehazi his servant, "Call this Shunammite woman." When he had called her, she stood before him.

And he said to him, "Say now to her, 'Look, you have been concerned for us with all this care. What can I do for you? Do you want me to speak on your behalf to the king or to the commander of the army?' " She answered, "I dwell among my own people."

So he said, "What then is to be done for her?" And Gehazi answered, "Actually, she has no son, and her husband is old."

And he said, "Call her." When he had called her, she stood in the doorway.

Then he said, "About this time next year you shall embrace a son." And she said, "No, my lord. Man of God, do not lie to your maidservant!"

2 Kings 4:8-16

The Shunammite woman and her husband were old and had not been able to have children, but the prophet of God spoke by the Holy Spirit. **"...the woman conceived, and bore a son when the appointed time had come, of which Elisha had told her"** (2 Kings 4:17).

There may be an area in your life where it looks like there will never be a harvest, a return or provision. But the good news is, you can sow the things you have and believe God to multiply them back in the form of your need, whatever it may be.

Perhaps you have been satisfied with living on a few of God's blessings, but God, by His Spirit, is calling you to walk in the abundant life which He has provided for you in His Word. He is calling you to rise up and lay hold of all of His promises, all of His provision, everything He has, for the world is watching you.

As the world sees you and your family abound in joy, love, health, finances and in every area of life, they will see God's glory and be drawn to His light.

You will have more than enough to give as the Holy Spirit leads you. The key is to get into a continual flow or rhythm of giving, realizing that you can never outgive God and you'll never be diminished!

Abundant Living Confessions

Here are eight Abundant Living Personalized Confessions from Chapter 7, which will help to move you into the mainstream of God's abundance:

1. God has opened the windows of heaven upon me, simply because I'm a tither (Malachi 3:10).
2. God will rebuke the devourer for me because I am a tither (Malachi 3:11).
3. Giving unto the Lord will not diminish me. Instead, it is God's avenue to increase me.
4. My harvest will be in proportion to my giving. The more I give, the more I will receive.
5. God will supply all my needs according to His riches in glory by Christ Jesus (Philippians 4:19).
6. Meeting the needs of the poor is part of a true fast. It is my responsibility to help meet their needs.
7. Because I consider the poor, I will be delivered in time of trouble. I will not be delivered over to the will of my enemies. I will be blessed, and I will be raised up from illness (Psalm 41:1-3).
8. I cannot outgive God. His rewards will exceed my giving.

CHAPTER 8
WATERING YOUR SEED

O nce you have planted your financial seeds or the seed of God's Word in your life, you need to mix faith with your seed.

Second Corinthians 4:13 explains the spirit of faith: **"And since we have the same spirit of faith, according to what is written, 'I *believed* and therefore I *spoke*,' we also *believe* and therefore *speak*."**

To mix faith with your seed is to *believe* the Word with your heart and *speak* it with your mouth. The believing and speaking are the planting, the watering and the sunshine that cause the seed to come forth and produce.

When you believe and say, "Jesus, I believe You were raised from the dead, and I confess You as my Lord and Savior," that seed comes forth and produces a born-again experience.

Everything in the Kingdom of God operates the same way. The spirit of faith, or the *believing* and *speaking*, are the two necessary ingredients to mix with the seed of the Word for a bountiful harvest to come forth.

The Word gives you the seed of healing that Jesus Christ bore your sicknesses and carried your diseases:

Surely He has borne our griefs and carried our sorrows; yet we esteemed Him stricken, smitten by God, and afflicted.

But He was wounded for our transgressions, He was bruised for our iniquities; the chastisement for our peace was upon Him, and by His stripes we are healed.

Isaiah 53:4,5

When you receive this Word in your heart and acknowledge it with your mouth, it will produce healing in your body.

The same principle works with peace. Hebrews 4:3 says, **"For we who have believed do enter that rest...."** God gives you seed in His Word for rest.

You must believe and speak God's Word before you will see the manifestation of His promises. As I began to understand this principle, I saw people who had been in church for years and knew all about the Bible, yet there was no fruit in their lives. Why? The spirit of faith is not just *knowing* about the Bible. It is the mixing — *believing* and *speaking* — that causes the Word to produce fruit.

When you plant the Word in someone, you can believe that the seed of the Word will produce. The story of Kenneth Copeland's salvation experience graphically portrays the power of the seed of the Word. Gloria had been saved. One day as Kenneth was lying on the couch in his living room, thinking about Gloria's salvation and what a blessing she was to him, suddenly he heard a voice he had heard some fifteen years earlier when he was a small boy. It was the voice of his Sunday school teacher who said, "Boys, if you are going to be saved and go to heaven, you must be born again."

At that moment, Kenneth acknowledged Jesus Christ as his Lord and Savior. The seed of the Word had been in him for years. As Gloria and others interceded for him, his heart was opened to hear the word of the Lord.

Another very touching example of the value of the seed of the Word is when Oral Roberts, as a teenage boy, was dying of tuberculosis. Doctors had given up on his recovery. They told him there was no hope. But his sister Jewel came to see him and spoke seven words that changed his life: *Oral, God is going to heal you.*

Oral had grown up in a preacher's home, but he said when he heard those seven words, that seed went into him and he began to believe for his healing. His brother came to him and said, "Oral, there is an evangelist in a nearby town who is preaching and people are getting healed. I am going to take you to him, and God is going to heal you."

They carried Oral to the meeting where a man of God laid his hands on him and rebuked the work of the devil in his life. Brother Roberts said, "I felt my lungs open up, and I could breathe without great effort for the first time in my life." He began to mend from that very hour.

The seed of his sister's seven words changed Brother Roberts' world. That seed went into his heart and worked in his life. Brother Roberts has stood before millions of people and said, "God is going to heal you" — all because one person dared to speak the word of faith into his life.

Your words carry awesome power for good or for evil. They carry power to water your seed or to dig it up.

Isaiah said God's Word would prosper. It would bring forth a harvest. It would not return void.

> **For as the rain comes down, and the snow from heaven, and do not return there, but water the earth, and make it bring forth and bud, that it may give seed to the sower and bread to the eater,**
> **So shall My word be that goes forth from My mouth; it shall not return to Me void, but it shall accomplish what I please, and it shall prosper in the thing for which I sent it.**
>
> **Isaiah 55:10,11**

The seed of God's Word will bring the harvest that He sent it forth to accomplish. When you hear the Word of God preached, it will feed you spiritually. The Word is food to eat, but it is also seed to sow.

When you hear the Word of God, you can say, "I am good ground. The Word is working in me. The seed of healing is growing inside me. I am redeemed from the curse. I am a new creation.

Old things have passed away. I am walking in liberty. Everlasting joy is on my head."

The watering of your financial seed is done in the same way. Speak God's Word over the seeds you have planted: "I am the head and not the tail. I am blessed coming in, and I am blessed going out. All the work of my hands is blessed. The Lord commands His blessings upon me. I will lend and not borrow. The Lord teaches me to profit and leads me in the way I should go."

Hold fast to the confession of your faith, for He is faithful Who promised (Hebrews 10:23).

You can cultivate the seed in your life. Every day you need to get your mixer going. When you're driving to work, begin to confess, "I am redeemed from the curse. I am healed by the stripes of Jesus. My steps are ordered, guided, directed and established by the Lord. Everywhere I go, I am led by the Spirit of God. I let the peace of God rule in my heart. All of my children are taught of the Lord, and they shall rise up and bless the Lord."

You can hear the seed of the Word all day long, but after you have heard it, you must believe it and speak it. That is your mixing.

To speak and stand upon God's Word means to *hear*, *believe*, *declare* and *do* God's Word. Build it into every area of your life. God says in Jeremiah 1:12 KJV, **"...I will hasten my word to perform it."**

Second Chronicles 16:9 says, **"For the eyes of the Lord run to and fro throughout the whole earth, to show Himself strong on behalf of those whose heart is loyal to Him...."**

If you have been standing on the Word for your finances, don't give up. The Word is working.

Between my sophomore and junior year at Oral Roberts University, I was offered a job in the oil fields where I had worked two summers before. I spent all the money I had to go to O.R.U.

my first semester in January, 1972, and I had two more years to complete.

At the end of my first semester at O.R.U., a door opened for me to work with the youth in a church in Arkansas. This position didn't pay very much. I would have to pay room and board, and the salary was about half of what I would earn working in the oil fields. If I worked in the oil fields, I would also be living at home, eating Mom's good cooking! Yet, God dealt with me about working for Him instead of working for my needs.

It was a big decision because if I saved all the money I would make ministering to the youth, it wouldn't even pay half of one semester at O.R.U. that fall. I decided to work as a summer youth director and I turned down the oil field job.

I prayed, "God, You've got to come through." He assured me, "If you will work for Me and do what you do as unto Me, you will never lack in any area of your life."

Everything worked out for the summer. Mrs. Davis, the woman in whose home I stayed, was in her eighties. She only charged $7.00 a week for board and $5.00 a week for lunch. She had one of those old-fashioned boarding homes where anyone in the community could come and eat dinner with her. She always had a big plate of fried chicken, mashed potatoes, gravy and homemade rolls. Someone even paid for my food and room.

By late July, I still had no money for my tuition at O.R.U. I had been accepted, but I didn't know where I would get the money. One thing I've learned over the years, God is never late! The miracles I needed came in two different letters from O.R.U. The first letter said I had received an academic scholarship which would cover half of the cost of my tuition, room and board for an entire year. The other letter related to my application to work in the O.R.U. men's dorm as a resident advisor.

That spring I had not been selected as a resident advisor for the fall, which is where I felt I was to be. No one knew me, and there were more than sixty applicants for twenty R.A. positions.

The second letter from O.R.U. came from the Dean's office where a friend, Don Shields, had been hired as Assistant Dean. One of the students who had been selected as a R.A. for the fall semester joined the Navy, which created an opening. It was through Don's recommendation (he and I had worked together in the P.E. laundry during the spring semester) that I was selected for the vacant R.A. position. That was the other half of my school costs. They were paid in full for the new academic year by mid-July.

God has proven Himself over and over in my life since I made the decision to go with Him and do what He wanted me to do.

The time between sowing and reaping is a time of trusting God to multiply the seed you have sown as you continually water it with the confession of His Word.

Abundant Living Confessions

Here are seven Abundant Living Personalized Confessions from Chapter 8, which will help to move you into the mainstream of God's abundance:

1. To mix faith with the seed of God's Word or with the financial seeds I have sown is to *believe* the Word in my heart and *speak* it with my mouth.
2. My words carry awesome power for good or for evil.
3. God's Word will not return void, but it will bring forth a harvest in my life as I believe it, speak it and become a doer of it (Isaiah 55:10,11).
4. To speak God's Word over the financial seeds I have planted will bring forth a multiplied harvest.
5. I will not grow weary in doing good or lose heart, for in due season I will reap (Galatians 6:9).
6. God hastens to perform His Word in my life (Jeremiah 1:12).
7. As I serve God with my life and go in the way the Holy Spirit leads me, God will supply all of my needs.

CHAPTER 9

God Takes Pleasure in
Your Prosperity

**Let the Lord be magnified, who has pleasure in the
prosperity of His servant.**

Psalm 35:27

It is the devil who wants to rip you off, but it is God Who
wants to bless you. Jesus came so we could have life in all
its fullness. Many people are still messed up in their thinking as to the goodness of God and the evil of the devil.

Most people want their children to be as blessed as they
are, or even more so. How dare we accuse God of having less
compassion than a human being! God's name and His character
have been maligned by religion that has said, "God wants people
poor and beat down." That is *not* true. And neither is spirituality
synonymous with poverty and lack.

My Father God is a good Father, and Jesus is a good
Shepherd to His sheep. Jesus identified the thief and the destroyer in John 10:10 so we could get our thinking straight. God
is always the Giver of good and perfect gifts (James 1:17).

The book of Job reveals three primary things about Job's
life:

1. God blessed Job.
2. The devil attacked him.
3. God restored him.

If you can understand this pattern in Job's life, you can understand the rest of the Book: *God blesses and restores, but the
devil attacks and destroys.*

Many people are lost in the woods over God's blessings. They don't know where good things come from, and they don't know where bad things come from. You can't resist the devil if you don't know who he is. You can't resist bad things if you think God is giving them to you.

It's not God Who is sending poverty into India or Haiti or Mozambique or any other area. That's the devil's job. You go to any poverty area or ghetto in our country and you'll find drugs, crime, immorality and uncleanness. Drugs and crime aren't limited to these areas, but they fester in these places.

Sharon and I have been in some of the poorest countries in the world. We've been in places where we've seen little kids coming out of very modest homes where there's trash, junk, dump and sewer all around the other houses, but they have been born again and they are right with God. They come out of those houses wearing shirts and britches that are neat, clean and pressed and nice shoes. What makes the difference? God will prosper His people right in the middle of poverty!

God wants to bless all of His people, but some have their arms folded. It's time to acknowledge, "Lord, if You made the whole universe for me, then I'm going to receive what You have for me." Once He can get His blessings to you, then you can begin to bless the world. If you don't have anything, how can you give anything?

We've got to begin to have faith for prosperity for a purpose. In other words, if you get full of the Holy Ghost, you can give some of Him to someone else. If you're dry as a bone and you don't have any power in your life, when someone needs prayer for healing, they won't come to you. They'll look for a person who is overflowing with the life of God. If you've got the joy of the Lord and the peace of God, you can share it with someone else.

Conditions for Receiving God's Best Blessings

Psalm, chapter 1, talks about the blessings of the Lord. **"Blessed is the man who walks not in the counsel of the ungodly..."** (v. 1). If you're listening to ungodliness, reading it, or fellowshipping with it, you will not prosper.

"...nor stands in the path of sinners..." (v. 1). If you are doing the same thing sinners are doing, you'll not be blessed. We are to love sinners, but he is talking about not hooking up with their ways.

The blessed person does not sit **"...in the seat of the scornful"** (v. 1). A *scorner* is a faultfinder, a mocker, a criticizer, a person who can find all the little sticks in someone else's eyes, but fails to see the telephone pole in his own! We need to know that scorners will not be blessed. Some people believe they have been anointed to be gap locators rather than gap standers!

"But his delight [the person who is blessed] **is in the law of the Lord, and in His law he meditates day and night"** (v. 2). To walk in the blessings of the Lord, you will need to delight yourself in the law of the Lord. His law is liberty. **"If you abide in My word, you are My disciples indeed. And you shall know the truth, and the truth shall make you free.... Therefore if the Son makes you free, you shall be free indeed"** (John 8:31,32,36).

The sum total of all of God's commandments is, **"...whatever you want men to do to you, do also to them..."** (Matthew 7:12). We call it the Golden Rule. We are to meditate day and night in the law of love.

"He shall be like a tree planted by the rivers of water, that brings forth its fruit in its season..." (Psalm 1:3). Instead of an old, dried up branch, you will be blessed and you will be a fruit producer.

"...whose leaf also shall not wither..." (v. 3). The leaves of a tree that is planted where there is no water will eventually wither. But if you are planted in the rivers of living water (God in you, the Word in you), your leaf will not wither.

When everyone else is famished, weak and intimidated, you will keep bearing fruit. If you are in the riverbed of God's Word, you will bear fruit that remains continually.

The last part of verse 3, Psalm, chapter 1, says, "**And whatever he does shall prosper.**" Everything your hand touches, because you are a disciple (a learner) of God's Word, *will prosper.* We're talking about living in God's abundance. Begin to say: "Whatever my hand touches prospers. I am delighting myself in the Lord."

God wants you to prosper and be blessed, but there are conditions to be met. You can't be bad-mouthing, running in sin, or not spending any time in the Word and in prayer, and expect to be blessed. You need to stay in communion with God.

God's Favor

Psalm, chapter 5, verses 11,12 say:

But let all those rejoice who put their trust in You; let them ever shout for joy, because You defend them; let those also who love Your name be joyful in You.

For You, O Lord, will bless the righteous; with favor You will surround him as with a shield.

One of the primary keys to walking in abundance is to get a revelation that *God's abundance is for you.* It is God's will that you prosper.

No Want to Those Who Seek the Lord

Because of not understanding this, some people are gripped with fear about how they are going to pay their light bill. I got to thinking about how much it would cost to supply the water for Niagara Falls, the Mississippi, Nile, Amazon and Danube rivers, and God does it. Then I got to thinking about how much it would cost to light a star. Do you think God is worried about paying energy bills? God has so much more than we have ever dreamed or tapped into.

Psalm 34:7-10 will help you understand God's covenant promise of abundance for obedient believers:

> **The angel of the Lord encamps all around those who fear Him, and delivers them.**
>
> **Oh, taste and see that the Lord is good; blessed is the man who trusts in Him!** [A lot of people have "things," but they've also got pain, heartache, turmoil, confusion and worry because their trust is in their "things" rather than in the Lord.]
>
> **Oh, fear the Lord, you His saints!** *There is no want to those who fear Him.*
>
> **The young lions lack and suffer hunger; but those who seek the Lord shall not lack any good thing.**

The movers and shakers who trust in their riches will come to a place of lack.

In 1973 Sharon and I were married, and we believed God for an apartment for $65 a month. God gave us exactly what we had believed for in a garage apartment, bills paid.

At that time, we only had one car and we were on different schedules. We both attended O.R.U., but Sharon worked at the school and I worked in a local church each afternoon. A city bus had never gone by the area of our apartment, but routes were changed and that fall they made a stop right in front of our apartment. The bus company only had one route that went to and from O.R.U. and this was it! Because of Sharon's schedule, many days she needed the car, and I was able to take the bus to our apartment and walk to work.

We came to a time when I had to begin making hospital visits, so I needed a vehicle. My brother Charles called and said, "I'm being transferred to Clark Air Force Base in the Philippines. I will be there for about a year and a half. Could you keep my car for me during this time?"

The day Charles brought his big Bonneville Pontiac to us, he also pulled a MasterCard out of his pocket and said, "I'll pay for all the gas and oil and repairs." You may be thinking, "That wasn't the Lord. That was your brother!" I have a question for you: When was the last time your brother gave you a car and a credit card to use? It came exactly when we needed it.

God takes pleasure in blessing us with His provision. Sharon and I thanked God every day we drove Charles' car. Every time people get blessed and they realize it is God Who is blessing them and they thank Him, God is magnified.

Now, let's look at Psalm 36:7,8:

How precious is Your lovingkindness, O God! Therefore the children of men put their trust under the shadow of Your wings.

They are abundantly satisfied with the fullness of Your house, and You give them drink from the river of Your pleasures ["the fullness of Your house" means abundant provision].

God is interested in your prosperity. He wants to bless and prosper you beyond your wildest imaginations!

Abundant Living Confessions

Here are nine Abundant Living Personalized Confessions from Chapter 9, which will help to move you into the mainstream of God's abundance:

1. God wants me blessed. He takes pleasure in my prosperity (Psalm 35:27).
2. God is the Giver of good and perfect gifts and abundant life. But Satan has come to steal, kill and destroy. Neither of their characteristics will ever change. God is forever *good*, while the devil is forever *evil* (James 1:17; John 10:10).
3. I am receiving God's blessings so I can be a blessing to others.

4. Because I walk in the counsel of the godly, I am blessed (Psalm 1:1).
5. My delight is in God's Word. I meditate in it day and night. As a result, I am a bearer of fruit that remains (Psalm 1:2; John 15:16).
6. The truth of God's Word makes me free (John 8:32).
7. Because I am consistent in studying, meditating and obeying God's Word, I am prospering in everything He leads me to do.
8. God surrounds me with favor as with a shield (Psalm 5:12).
9. Because I daily seek the Lord and I am in relationship with Him, I do not lack any good thing (Psalm 34:10).

CHAPTER 10

Believing for the Hundredfold Return

Give, and it will be given to you: good measure, pressed down, shaken together, and running over will be put into your bosom. For with the same measure that you use, it will be measured back to you.

Luke 6:38

Your harvest will always be proportionate to the seed that you plant. The same yardstick you use in measuring out the seed in planting and giving will be the same yardstick used to multiply the harvest back to you.

If you plant one seed, then that's the guideline by which your harvest will be multiplied back to you. But if the number of seeds you plant is increased, then the multiplication back to you will also be increased.

Charles and Frances Hunter used a tiny plastic coffee spoon they received from the airlines to demonstrate this principle: *The measure you give will be the measure you receive.* A hundred scoops with that little spoon wouldn't be very much. If you give in that proportion, you will receive a similar return. As the size of the spoon increases, your harvest will increase.

Jesus said, **"Most assuredly, I say to you, unless a grain of wheat falls into the ground and dies, it remains alone; but if it dies, it produces much grain"** (John 12:24).

God planted Jesus in the earth as a seed. He wanted the human race, including you and me, so He used the laws of seedtime and harvest to get us. He gave the best seed that He had, His only begotten Son. When that seed comes up in your life, it comes up in the exact likeness and kind of the first seed that was planted. When you were born again, you were made in the exact image and likeness of Jesus Christ. If you could see your own spirit, it looks just like Jesus. **"...If anyone is in Christ, he is a new creation..."** (2 Corinthians 5:17).

God expected a return when He gave Jesus. He didn't say, "I think I'll just give My Son and whatever will be will be!" No, He predetermined the results that would come forth. When Jesus hung on the cross, He saw you and me. He had a vision by faith of the world being drawn into His Kingdom.

In the spring, nurseries sell little packets of seeds for planting. On the seed packets are pictures of the harvest. Every time you plant, you ought to get a vision of the harvest you expect to receive.

When a farmer plants corn seed, he isn't thinking of it coming up in seed. He sees the full corn in the ear. You need to see the results the moment you plant. That's what it means to call things that are not as though they already were (Romans 4:17). God always speaks the end from the beginning.

In Genesis 3:15, God told Satan that the seed of woman would crush his head. God was speaking the end from the beginning. He was calling things that were not as though they already were. In the mind of God, Jesus' birth, life and triumph over the devil in physical death and resurrection were already accomplished. He was letting Satan know ahead of time that a triumphant, overcoming Seed was coming.

You will get exactly what you say. This is also true of what you see. If you say that you are healed by the stripes of Jesus, but in your mind you have a mental picture of always being sick, you have one law operating against another. God wants you to cast down imaginations and bring every thought into obedience to His Word (2 Corinthians 10:5 KJV). Your heart believes you are healed by the stripes of Jesus because the Word has been sown. Then *see* yourself walking in wholeness.

When I teach on healing, usually I say, "*See* yourself getting up. *See* yourself whole." Your mind receives a mental image, just like the pictures on those packets of seeds.

The Hundredfold Return

So Jesus answered and said, "Assuredly, I say to you, there is no one who has left house or brothers or sisters or father or mother or wife or children or lands, for My sake and the gospel's, who shall not receive a hundredfold now in this time — houses and brothers and sisters and mothers and children and lands, with persecutions — and in the age to come, eternal life."

Mark10: 29,30 NKJV

Whatever you sow, you can believe for the hundredfold return on it. This is a law of God, so you should expect it to work in your life.

The hundredfold return was first revealed in the Old Testament. There was a famine in Canaan where the Philistines inhabited the land. God had given Abraham all the land he could see to the north, south, east and west, but the Philistines were still there.

Because of the famine in the land of Canaan, Isaac said, "I want to go down to Egypt and get out of this situation. I want to go where I can plant something and believe for it to grow." But God said:

"Do not go down to Egypt; live in the land of which I shall tell you.

"Dwell in this land, and I will be with you and bless you; for to you and your descendants I give all these lands, and I will perform the oath which I swore to Abraham your father.

"And I will make your descendants multiply as the stars of heaven; I will give to your descendants all these lands; and in your seed all the nations of the earth shall be blessed;

"Because Abraham obeyed My voice and kept My charge, My commandments, My statutes, and My laws."

Then Isaac sowed in that land, and *reaped in the same year a hundredfold;* and the Lord blessed him.

Genesis 26:2-5,12

Imagine a hundredfold harvest in a one-year period! God blessed Isaac in the midst of a famine. Some people have said that the message of prosperity and the hundredfold return will only work in America. If that's true, then how do you explain the hundredfold return for Isaac in the midst of a severe famine in the Middle East?

The message of giving to God and the hundredfold return is exactly what is needed in lands of famine. The reason there has been such a failure in certain countries is because people have given their worship to heathen idols. Thank God that believers in Jesus Christ are rising up all over the earth, even in lands of famine. They are being blessed, and they are teaching others how to be blessed.

Sowing the Eternal Seed of God's Word

"Heaven and earth will pass away, but My words will by no means pass away" (Matthew 24:35).

God's Word is eternal seed. It has the capacity of reproducing itself in a magnificent way. We need to understand the laws of giving and receiving concerning the Word of God and the potential of that seed to produce in our lives.

You were born again through the incorruptible seed of the Word of God. **"Having been born again, not of corruptible seed but incorruptible, through the word of God which lives and abides forever"** (1 Peter 1:23).

God's Word is an incorruptible seed. It cannot be destroyed, but it will endure forever. The seeds of man — his thoughts, ideologies and philosophies — will perish. Like the grass of the field, they will wither and die.

One day God planted a seed in a young girl named Mary. She believed and received that seed and released her faith. The Word won't work unless you mix it with faith, and seeds won't work if they just sit in a dry place. They have to be planted in fertile soil.

The seed of the Word was planted in the fertile soil of Mary's heart. She mixed faith with that seed and said, **"Let it be to me according to your word"** (Luke 1:38). The miracle was on!

God is Spirit, and when you are born again, God places His nature inside of you. Through the precious promises of God, you become a partaker of His divine nature (2 Peter 1:4). Through partaking of the seed of God's Word, He reproduces Himself in you.

The Bible says we are like a small seed: first the blade, then the ear, then the full corn in the ear (Mark 4:28 KJV). The Word grows in us as we continually partake of it.

Abundant Living Confessions

Here are three Abundant Living Personalized Confessions from Chapter 10, which will help to move you into the mainstream of God's abundance:

1. Like Isaac who obeyed God and sowed in a time of famine and received a hundredfold blessing from the Lord *in the same year*, I will sow regardless of economic conditions and expect to receive the hundredfold harvest in the same year.
2. Obedience to God is the key to my prosperity.
3. I am a partaker of God's divine nature by reading, studying and meditating upon His Word (2 Peter 1:4).

CHAPTER 11

LIFTING THE LID OFF YOUR THINKING!

ow big is your God? He has unlimited ability, yet in some people's minds, He has very little ability.

Who is with you in this life? Are you on your own, or is the King of the universe living with you? If the King of the universe is living with you, why not act like it? He wants to do the same thing today He did 2,000 years ago. Scripture says He **"is the same yesterday, today, and forever"** (Hebrews 13:8).

Colossians 1:27 says, **"Christ in you, the hope of glory."** Although Jesus is seated at the right hand of the Father, He is in you through the presence of the Holy Spirit.

Jesus said, **"If anyone loves Me, he will keep My word; and My Father will love him, and We will come to him and make Our home with him"** (John 14:23). First Corinthians 6:19 says, **"Or do you not know that your body is the temple of the Holy Spirit *who is in you*, whom you have from God, and you are not your own?"** The Holy Spirit lives inside of those who love God and keep His commandments.

What God spoke in Genesis 1 is still for today: **"Be fruitful and multiply; fill the earth and subdue it; have dominion"** (v. 28). Verses 29-31 say:

> **And God said, "See, I have given you every herb that yields seed which is on the face of all the earth, and every tree whose fruit yields seed; to you it shall be for food.**
>
> **"Also, to every beast of the earth, to every bird of the air, and to everything that creeps on the earth, in which there is life, I have given every green herb for food"; and it was so.**

Then God saw everything that He had made, and indeed it was very good...."

When God planned and created the earth, He had you and me in mind. The devil does not own this planet. Psalm 24:1 says, **"The earth is the Lord's, and all its fullness...."** In Haggai 2:8 God says, **"The silver is Mine, and the gold is Mine."** The cattle on a thousand hills are His (Psalm 50:10), and the oil and gas under those hills are His, too. He owns it all.

When Jesus Christ paid for your salvation, He also paid for your provision and for your health. Psalm 84:11 says, **"...No good thing will He withhold from those who walk uprightly."**

Some people say God is against "things." If He is against our having "things," why is He adding them to those who serve Him? Food, clothing, shelter and all the things that people in the world are trying to get, God said, would be added to those who **"seek first the kingdom of God and His righteousness..."** (Matthew 6:33). God is not against things, but He is against us putting our trust in "things," and living for them, which is vanity, futility and emptiness.

Deuteronomy, chapter 8, speaks of the abundance the Lord desires for us to have:

For the Lord your God is bringing you into a good land, a land of brooks of water, of fountains and springs, that flow out of valleys and hills;

A land of wheat and barley, of vines and fig trees and pomegranates, a land of olive oil and honey;

A land in which *you will eat bread without scarcity, in which you will lack nothing;* a land whose stones are iron and out of whose hills you can dig copper.

When you have eaten and are full, then you shall bless the Lord your God for the good land which He has given you.

Beware that you do not forget the Lord your God by not keeping His commandments, His judgments, and His statutes which I command you today,

> Lest — when you have eaten and are full, and have built beautiful houses and dwell in them;
>
> And when your herds and your flocks multiply, and your silver and your gold are multiplied, and all that you have is multiplied;
>
> When your heart is lifted up, and you forget the Lord your God who brought you out of the land of Egypt, from the house of bondage;
>
> Who led you through that great and terrible wilderness, in which were fiery serpents and scorpions and thirsty land where there was no water; who brought water for you out of the flinty rock;
>
> Who fed you in the wilderness with manna, which your fathers did not know, that He might humble you and that He might test you, to do you good in the end —
>
> Then you say in your heart, "My power and the might of my hand have gained me this wealth."
>
> **Deuteronomy 8:7-17**

In other words, God is saying, "Do not say, 'It is in my own ability, power, intelligence, education and hard work that I have gained this wealth.' "

Verses 18 and 19 of Deuteronomy, chapter 8, say:

> And you shall remember the Lord your God, for it is He who gives you power to get wealth, that He may establish His covenant which He swore to your fathers, as it is this day.
>
> Then it shall be, if you by any means forget the Lord your God, and follow other gods, and serve them and worship them, I testify against you this day that you shall surely perish.

Since God is the One Who gives us the power to get wealth, He is not against our having "things."

The Israelites forgot their source of wealth. The prophet Malachi told them:

"Will a man rob God? Yet you have robbed Me! But
you say, 'In what way have we robbed You?' In tithes and
offerings.

"You are cursed with a curse, for you have robbed
Me, even this whole nation."

Malachi 3:8,9

The prophet Haggai said:

"...he who earns wages, earns wages to put into a bag
with holes."

Thus says the Lord of hosts: "Consider your ways!

"Go up to the mountains and bring wood and build
the temple, that I may take pleasure in it and be glorified,"
says the Lord.

"You looked for much, but indeed it came to little;
and when you brought it home, I blew it away. Why?"
says the Lord of hosts. "Because of My house that is in
ruins, while every one of you runs to his own house.

"Therefore the heavens above you withhold the dew,
and the earth withholds its fruit."

Haggai 1:6-10

Notice, they were to build God's house *first*, then God
would build their individual houses. This is in agreement with
Matthew 6:33: **"But seek first the kingdom of God and His
righteousness, and all these things shall be added to you."**

The prophet Malachi goes on:

"Bring all the tithes into the storehouse, that there
may be food in My house, and try Me now in this," says
the Lord of hosts, "If I will not open for you the windows
of heaven and pour out for you such blessing that there
will not be room enough to receive it.

"And I will rebuke the devourer for your sakes, so
that he will not destroy the fruit of your ground, nor shall
the vine fail to bear fruit for you in the field," says the
Lord of hosts;

> **"And all nations will call you blessed, for you will be
> a delightful land," says the Lord of hosts.**
>
> **Malachi 3:10-12**

If we keep our eyes on Jesus, continue to serve God and
keep giving to Him and to the needy and the hurting, God will
take us higher and increase us more and more.

Deuteronomy 28:47,48 says:

> **Because you did not serve the Lord your God with
> joy and gladness of heart, for the abundance of everything,
> Therefore you shall serve your enemies....**

This makes it clear that it is God Who gives you the
abundance of all things. It's time to make a decision that you're
not going to serve the devil and you're not going to live for the
world. Then change your thinking from a lack mentality to an
abundance mentality.

When God asks a person to do something who has a lack
mentality, usually their first response is, "I can't do that," and
they begin to list the reasons:

- "I don't have the strength."
- "I don't have the ability."
- "I don't have the time."
- "I don't have the money."

How big is your God? What has He told you to do? What
are His plans for your life?

R. G. LeTourneau was a common laborer, but God began
to speak to him in the nighttime, giving him ideas about the
invention of earth-moving equipment. He would draw what he
saw, and he began to patent those machines, manufacture them
and sell them.

LeTourneau was a born-again Christian. He began giving
10 percent to God and as God increased him, he gave 20 percent. Then he got a vision of putting the Gospel in different
nations and he started giving 30 percent. The day came when
he was giving 40 percent of his income. He kept seeking

91

God and serving Him, acknowledging that it was God Who gave him the power to get wealth.

The day came when LeTourneau gave 90 percent of his income to the work of God and lived off of 10 percent. How would you like to be increased to that point? As you serve the Lord, He will increase you.

Romans 8:31,32 says:

> **What then shall we say to these things? If God is for us, who can be against us?**
>
> **He who did not spare His own Son, but delivered Him up for us all, how shall He not with Him also freely give us all things?**

A young couple from Europe came to America and saw Christian television. It became their dream to take Christian television back to Europe. They talked to people who had satellite time available, and to make a long story short, with miraculous favor, this young couple in their twenties, have put Christian television in Europe. We're on the air there, along with Kenneth Copeland, Benny Hinn, Jesse Duplantis, and others. Today we're hearing from people from all over Europe.

What happened? Two people heard from God and they said, "Our God is big enough to do it." What is your dream? Some people's potential is locked up because they've had a lack mentality. *It's time to lift the lid off your thinking!*

Where there is a vision and a will, God will make a way. If you can believe it and conceive it, you can receive it. If you cannot believe it and conceive it in your mind, you cannot receive it in your life. Some people think, "If God wants that to happen, He'll just drop it on me." No, He's going to work through your faith.

Abraham had to believe and take a walk to inherit the promised land. Everyone who has ever received a miracle had to do something.

Tom Newman, president and founder of Impact Productions, had a dream to reach a sight and sound generation through the drama, "Toymaker," which has been performed around the world for seventeen years. Then Tom began to share with me about another dream to make Christian movies which would touch the world. We began to agree on it in prayer. His premier movie, "Resurrection," came out at Eastertime, 1998.

It costs several thousands of dollars to produce a quality movie. How did Tom move from being a schoolteacher with a play to becoming a movie producer? He didn't get there with a lack mentality! He had to believe that God is a God Who is more than enough and that God would make a way.

When Sharon and I had a desire to have a Christian camp, in the natural there was no way because we were in the middle of a church building program. But God began to deal with me to believe for it and release my faith.

We wrote it down and agreed on it in prayer: "Land on a lake; thirty minutes from Tulsa; paved roads, electricity, sewer and water already in place; for free; Mark 11:24." Today Camp Victory is a reality. It is on Lake Keystone, thirty minutes from Tulsa, with paved roads and electricity, sewer and water already in place, and we got it for free. (We pay $1.00 a year to lease it, and someone gave the money for it.)

Today we also have dorm space for over a hundred kids, one of the most beautiful pavilions that will seat about 600 people, and a swimming pool.

There was a time when my mind was thinking, "It can never happen." But then our faith arose and we envisioned a place where we could take the children who regularly come to our church, plus the children from the government-subsidized apartment communities who would never have an opportunity to go to a Christian camp. Today it is happening.

It is through *an understanding of God's love for you* that He is able to do exceedingly abundantly above all that you ask or think (Ephesians 3:20). When we understand how much God loves us, then we know that He wants to bless us so we can be a blessing in the earth and a light to the nations. Dr. Lester Sumrall used to say to me, "There's no bottom to God's barrel."

When Bernis Duke took over the Oral Roberts University tennis program, he faced the dilemma of how to recruit top-notch tennis players. He began to pray and God gave him an idea to send post cards with a picture of the O.R.U. Prayer Tower and campus on it to outstanding high school tennis players. He sent cards to South Africa, Rhodesia, Yugoslavia, the Czech Republic, and other nations of the world.

By the time I arrived on campus in 1972, O.R.U. ranked number three in the nation in tennis. O.R.U. had recruited some of the best tennis players in the world. The young men receiving the cards were attracted to the Prayer Tower and to the campus. The coach would say, "If you're interested in a tennis scholarship, please contact me." Young men from the Communist countries were enrolled in Oral Roberts University's tennis program when I was an O.R.U. student.

When someone dares to believe God, regardless of their profession, God will make a way for them to receive His best!

The singles' ministry directors at Victory, Sherry and David Whisner, had a vision of feeding people and providing food, particularly for singles. They put a little tract together, put it in a small bag and placed it on several doorknobs in our city, with the instructions: "If you want to donate food for the needy, fill this bag and leave it on your front porch. We'll pick it up on (specified a day), and distribute it to needy people."

One man who received this packet said, "I think I'll give $40,000." Not only did he want to give food, but he wanted to provide jackets for little kids. With his money we bought 2,000 starter jackets for kids, which normally retail between $60 to $80 each. We were able to get them at a greatly reduced price.

Jesus made a difference in several children's lives because people with a vision dared to believe!

Do you have a vision or a dream that you would like to see the Lord explode? Have you had a lid on it? Maybe you've put a lid on someone else's dream. It's time to take the lid of limitation off of God!

Abundant Living Confessions

Here are ten Abundant Living Personalized Confessions from Chapter 11, which will help to move you into the mainstream of God's abundance:

1. Since Jesus is the same yesterday, today and forever, He wants to do for me today what He did 2,000 years ago (Hebrews 13:8).

2. Christ lives in me through the presence of the Holy Spirit (Colossians 1:27).

3. My body is the temple of the Holy Spirit (1 Corinthians 6:19).

4. No good thing will the Lord withhold from me, because I walk uprightly in obedience to His will (His Word) (Psalm 84:11).

5. The Lord gives me the power to get wealth, that He may establish His covenant with me (Deuteronomy 8:18).

6. As I bring my tithes into the storehouse (the church where I am fed spiritually), and offerings for other ministry, God will open the windows of heaven and pour out such a blessing upon me, I won't have room enough to receive it (Malachi 3:10).

7. As a tither, Jesus will also rebuke the devourer for my sake (Malachi 3:11).

8. I'm lifting the lid off my thinking today, because I now believe God is big enough to support the things He

has asked me to do. He is a Waymaker, and He is always more than enough for any need I face.

9. I'm believing, as Dr. Lester Sumrall did, "There's no bottom to God's barrel."

10. I can make a difference in this world through my obedience to God!

CHAPTER 12

GOD'S PURPOSE IN BLESSING YOU

G od's purpose for blessing His people is so we can bless the whole world with the Gospel of Jesus Christ. Through deceit, intellectualism and hard work, many people are pursuing "things" and "possessions" rather than God.

The blessing I am talking about is God's blessing that will enable you *to be a blessing*. I'm talking about the Proverbs 10:22 blessing: **"The blessing of the Lord makes one rich, and He adds no sorrow with it."** I'm talking about the Matthew 6:33 type of blessing: **"But seek first the kingdom of God and His righteousness, and** *all these things* **shall be added to you."**

When you are delivered from the power of sin, sickness, poverty and torment, you can begin to be a blessing to others.

Here's a testimony from one of our Victory Bible Institute students who volunteered in our ministry and headed up a cell group:

"I volunteer in the Personal Ministry Department. A call came in from a young woman who was in such a state of depression that she could not leave her house to come in for an appointment. She had a broken heart as a result of her husband's death seven years earlier. Jesus is the healer of the brokenhearted, so I shared Jesus' love and healing with her on the phone several times and invited her to my cell group. She wasn't ready to come out of her house yet.

"I had a breakfast planned at a restaurant for my cell group and I invited her. She came and afterwards began coming to the cell meetings. As she received the Word and the love in the cell group, she began to improve.

"During this time she was diagnosed with liver cancer and was scheduled for a biopsy. We prayed for her healing. The next week she went in for a cat scan, which revealed 'no cancer' in her liver. The biopsy was not needed.

"Depression tried to set in again, so I told her, 'Get up out of your chair and come to the cell meeting.' She came and was ministered to by the entire group. The following week she received the baptism of the Holy Spirit. She went home and began unpacking boxes that had been sitting in her house for over a year since her move."

This was a woman who was unable to function until the depression was broken off of her life. She was delivered from depression and healed of cancer because of one believer who acknowledged and walked in her inheritance and authority as the seed of Abraham. God intends for you to pass His blessings which come to you on to others.

The Body of Christ all over the world has simultaneously moved into the supernatural provision of God, because God is in a hurry to reach a generation of lost people who are sick, bound and hurting.

This is the hour for us to take the Gospel to the ends of the earth, to go places where we've never gone, to reach people who are unreached and to see the Body of Christ come out of debt.

R. W. Schambach challenged people to believe God for $2,000 to contribute to our land and building projects and to tithe on that amount in advance. He asked us to plant a tithe of $200 and believe God to bring in the rest. Sharon and I each planted $200. Within three days, $4,000 came into our hands to give. We stood in amazement as God supernaturally brought the money to us and to many others.

Proverbs 13:22 says, **"...the wealth of the sinner is stored up for the righteous."** The sinner's riches are going to be transferred in this end-time hour into the hands of people who will give it to reach the lost and to build up the Kingdom of God.

You may be unable to figure out how to get out of $100,000 worth of debt. When you plant $100, $1,000, or any other amount, start believing God for the hundredfold harvest in the same twelve-month period.

Many people have planted seed, but they have not released faith with it to expect a harvest. God will direct what you should give, which is between you and the Lord. I'm talking about seeing your faith loosed to believe God to get out of debt.

In Joel 2:29 God says, **"I will pour out My Spirit in those days."** He also says, **"And I will restore to you the years that the locust hath eaten, the cankerworm, and the caterpiller, and the palmerworm..."** (Joel 2:25 KJV).

Many people have years that have been wasted because of bondage and oppression. I'm talking about total deliverance, not just financial, but getting back your children, your health, integrity, purity, honesty, holiness and godliness.

We needed $600,000 for a land purchase in February, 1998, and the Lord reminded us, "Plant seeds into the poor, the needy, hurting people and outreaches of other ministries that are touching lives that you are not reaching." We planted and we've never stopped. The Lord dealt with us, "The seed of that money will produce a greater harvest than the money that you are holding in your hand. If you turn it into seed, it's hundredfold money. But if you spend it, that's all it will go for." The money for the land came right on time.

When you have a need, it's time to plant a seed; then expect a hundredfold harvest in the same year. God is no respecter of persons. He did it for Isaac, and He will do it for you in this hour, regardless of your present circumstances.

God's intent is to bless you to make you a blessing. He doesn't want your name to rot and your memory to be forgotten (Proverbs 10:7 KJV). He wants to honor your name and through you bless the families of the earth, just as He did with Abraham.

Abundant Living Confessions

Here are four Abundant Living Personalized Confessions from Chapter 12, which will help to move you into the mainstream of God's abundance:

1. The blessing of the Lord makes me rich, and He adds no sorrow with it (Proverbs 10:22).
2. The wealth of the sinner is laid up for me (Proverbs 13:22).
3. God is restoring to me the years that Satan has stolen from my life (Joel 2:25).
4. I am blessed so I can be a blessing to support the spreading of the Gospel to the ends of the earth. My name will not rot as will the names of the wicked, but the memory of my name and my life will be blessed forever. I will be named among the "just" (Proverbs 10:7 KJV).

CHAPTER 13
FINANCIAL FREEDOM CONFESSIONS

H ere are thirty-one financial freedom confessions to lift you out of financial bondage, stress and oppression into total freedom in this area. As you meditate upon God's Word, which is the basis of these confessions, hear and obey what the Spirit speaks to you.

John 8:32 says, **"And you shall know the truth, and the truth shall make you free."** God's Word is truth, and through your meditation in it, you shall be made free.

Aligning your words with God's Word is a key to victory. Proverbs 18:21 says, **"Death and life are in the power of the tongue, and those who love it will eat its fruit."** Obedience to God's Word is crucial to attain financial freedom. In other words, as you confess God's Word and become a doer of it, over a process of time you will achieve financial liberty and be in a position for God to increase you more and more (Psalm 115:14). He wants you blessed so you can be a blessing.

1

Thank You for forgiving me, Father, for wrong decisions and for leaning to the world's system as my financial source. I acknowledge You, Father, as Jehovah Jireh, the God Who is more than enough, and the Source of my finances. I ask Your Son Jesus Christ to be the Ruler of all the finances which You entrust to me. Amen.

1 John 1:9

2

I now understand, Father, that it is Your will that I prosper and be in health, even as my soul prospers in the spiritual riches of Your Word.

I will study to show myself approved unto You, Lord. Because Your wisdom dominates me, I will rightly divide Your Word as applicable to every area of life, including my finances, in Jesus' name.

3 John 2
2 Timothy 2:15

3

Thank You, Father, that the fruit of self-control is maturing in my human spirit, particularly in financial decisions. I am not driven to spend money out of compulsion, but I am led by Your Spirit in all of my financial affairs, in Jesus' name. Amen.

Galatians 5:22,23 AMP

4

Thank You, Father, for turning my captivity first in the spiritual arena, and secondly in the financial arena, in Jesus' name.

You have filled my mouth with laughter and my tongue with singing. You have done great things for me, Lord, for which I am glad. Your joy has overtaken the despair that has tried to come upon me. Your riches have overtaken my lack. In you, Lord Jesus, I rejoice!

Thank You that Your goodness and mercy follow me all the days of my life!

Psalm 126
Psalm 23:6

5

I bless You, Lord, with everything that is within me. I'll not forget Your benefits — forgiveness; healing (spiritually, mentally, emotionally, physically, socially and financially); redemption from destruction; lovingkindness and tender mercies; satisfying my mouth with good things; and renewing my youth as the eagle.

Forever, O Lord, I will bless You for Your mercy and grace.

Thank You for daily loading me with Your benefits, in Jesus' name. Amen.

Psalm 68:19
Psalm 103:1-5

6

I honor You, Lord, with the substance of my finances and with the firstfruits of my increase, which is the tithe (the first 10 percent of my gross income). I give my tithe to the storehouse, the primary source of my spiritual nourishment.

In response to my obedience in giving of tithes, offerings and alms, You have rebuked the devourer from my life and have opened the windows of heaven to pour Your blessings upon me, Lord.

Thank You for blessing me with Your abundance so I can be a blessing, in Jesus' name. Amen.

Proverbs 3:9,10
Malachi 3:8-12

7

Because You have taught me to be faithful, Lord, I am abounding with Your blessings.

I have sought Your Kingdom and Your righteousness as the number one priority of my life, Lord. Therefore, You are adding to me everything that I need. Thank You!

Proverbs 28:20
Matthew 6:33

8

Father, You said in Your Word that if I will humble myself, pray, seek Your face and turn from my wicked ways, You will hear me, forgive my sin and heal my land. I come to You in humility, Lord, to pray and seek Your face and turn from any ways that are unlike You, and I ask You to heal my finances. Change me as You desire in every area of my life, but right now particularly in the financial area, Lord.

Thank You, Father, for supplying me with Your riches in glory by Christ Jesus so I can be a blessing to others and help propagate the Gospel to the ends of the earth. Amen.

2 Chronicles 7:14
Philippians 4:19

9

No good thing will You withhold from me, Lord, because I seek You and walk uprightly before You, in Jesus' name. Amen.

Psalm 34:10
Psalm 84:11

10

Father God, You are the One Who has given me power to get wealth. You are the total Source of my financial supply. You are the Source of every good and perfect gift, which includes financial freedom and prosperity.

Thank You for instilling within me a mind-set to accept Your financial provision, Lord, with motives that will cause me to appropriately distribute it to those in need of Your life, love and blessings, in Jesus' name. Amen.

Deuteronomy 8:18
James 1:17

11

I have been redeemed from the curse of the law through You, Lord Jesus, and Abraham's blessings are overtaking me.

Generational curses of lack and poverty or a poverty mentality are broken off of me through my acceptance of the work of Your shed blood, Lord Jesus.

I live to give that others might know You, Lord Jesus. Amen.

Galatians 3:13,14
Revelation 12:11

12

Father, You said of Abraham, **"For I know him, that he will command his children and his household after him, and they shall keep the way of the Lord, to do justice and judgment; that the Lord may bring upon Abraham that which he hath spoken of him."** Then in Genesis 24:1, You said, **"...The Lord had blessed Abraham in all things."**

Father, thank You for helping me to set my household in order so divine prosperity can be loosed upon my family, in Jesus' name.

Genesis 18:19 KJV
Genesis 24:1 KJV

13

Thank You, Father, for teaching me to profit and leading me in the way I should go, in Jesus' name.

Thank You for giving me witty inventions and ideas from which I can profit for the primary purpose of sharing the Good News of Jesus Christ with others.

Proverbs 8:12
Isaiah 48:17

14

Because I am Your servant and I am obedient to You, Lord, I am spending my days in prosperity and I am enjoying Your pleasures.

It is Your desire to give me the treasures of Your Kingdom, Father, financially as well as spiritually.

Heaven's resources are replacing the lack I have experienced, in Jesus' name. Hallelujah!

Job 36:11
Luke 12:32

15

Through faith and patience, I inherit the promises of Your Word, Lord.

I am not slothful, but I am diligent in the work You have given me to do, Lord. Therefore, I will stand before kings. You will cause me to ride upon the high places of the earth, Lord, because I delight myself in You and I am a good steward of the time, talents and finances You have entrusted to me.

Proverbs 12:27
Proverbs 22:29
Proverbs 24:33,34
Isaiah 58:14
Hebrews 6:12

16

As a doer of Your Word and as a bountiful giver of finances, encouragement, food, clothing and shelter to those in need, I am laying up treasures in heaven, Lord. Moth and rust cannot corrupt and thieves cannot steal these acts of love and generosity, in Jesus' name.

My heart is set upon You, Lord, to seek You first.

Matthew 6:19-21,33

17

In Jesus' name, covetousness is bound from me and godly contentment is loosed unto me.

I am not moved by what others have, but I am moved only by the direction of Your Spirit in distributing and saving the finances entrusted to me, in Jesus' name. Amen.

Hebrews 13:5

18

You said in Your Word, Lord, that the *love of money*, not money itself, is the root cause of all evil. I repent for allowing money to have a hold on me, Lord, leading me into foolish purchases, investments, and desires.

With Your help, Lord, I will pursue righteousness, godliness, faith, love, patience and meekness, in Jesus' name. Amen.

1 Timothy 6:10,11

19

You are increasing me and my seed more and more, Lord, and blessing us so we can bless others with Your provision and truth, satisfying both their natural and spiritual hunger.

You take pleasure in my prosperity, Lord. You want me blessed. You want my cup to overflow. You want me to experience life in all its fullness.

Psalm 35:27
Psalm 115:12-15

20

I have left houses and lands and family to follow You, Lord Jesus. Therefore, in this hour I will receive a hundredfold return of all I have given up, with persecutions which You have given me the power, authority and ability to overcome.

Thank You for teaching me how to live in heaven on earth now, in this hour, and later to enjoy eternal life with You, Lord Jesus. Hallelujah!

Mark 10:29,30

21

I am sowing bountifully as a cheerful giver, Lord, and I am reaping a harvest in like kind — bountiful.

Because of Your grace upon my life, Lord, I have sufficiency in all things so I am able to give into every good work.

Thank You, Lord, for multiplying the seeds I have sown and for increasing the fruits of my righteousness.

2 Corinthians 9:6-11

22

Thank You, Father, for commanding Your blessings upon me. Everything to which I place my hand in obedience to the destiny You have set before me is blessed of You, Lord.

I am plenteous in goods and in the fruit of my body. I am a lender, not a borrower, the head financially and not the tail, above and not beneath, in Jesus' name. Amen.

Deuteronomy 28:1-14

23

Father, thank You for teaching me to be a generous giver. Because I give in good measure, pressed down, shaken together and running over quantity, finances are coming to me in the same measure.

You were generous in giving Your best, Father — Your Son — so I am generous in giving You my life to use as You will, in Jesus' name. Amen.

Luke 6:38
John 3:16

24

Thank You for purifying my heart's motives and showing Yourself strong in my behalf, Lord.

In You, Lord Jesus, I am more than a conqueror in the financial realm, as well as in the other areas of my life.

2 Chronicles 16:9
Romans 8:37

25

Father, thank You for doing exceeding abundantly above all that I have asked or even thought, according to Your power which is working in me, in Jesus' name.

Thank You for loosing Your treasures upon me, Lord, so my life can be a testimony to others of Your goodness.

Ephesians 3:20

26

Because I am willing and obedient to do Your will, Father, I am eating the good of the land. I am enjoying Your abundance in every area of my life, in Jesus' name. Amen.

Isaiah 1:19
John 10:10

27

The wealth of the sinner has been stored up for me. It is being transferred into my hands in this hour, because I have become a channel through which You, Father, can bless others all over the world with the Good News of the Gospel, in Jesus' name.

Proverbs 13:22
Mark 16:15

28

I am flourishing spiritually and financially like a palm tree and growing like a cedar in Lebanon. I am bringing forth fruit for Your Kingdom, Lord, and I will continue to bring forth fruit in old age.

You are upright, Lord, and there is no unrighteousness in You. It is a privilege to know You, Lord, and to be Your servant, in Jesus' name. Amen.

Psalm 92:12-15

29

Thank You, Father, for leading me, Your child, by Your Spirit in every area of life, including the financial area.

Your blessings make me rich, and You add no sorrow with them, in Jesus' name. Amen.

Proverbs 10:22
Romans 8:14

30

In spite of the economic turmoil in the world, my finances are intact because Your wisdom and knowledge are the stability of my times, Lord.

I am a partaker of Your divine nature through the precious promises of Your Word, in Jesus' name. Amen.

Isaiah 33:6
2 Peter 1:4

31

The greatest riches I have ever received is the free gift of life in You, Lord Jesus, which freed me of the debt of sin.

Because You gave me righteousness for my unrighteousness, Lord Jesus, I have become Your workmanship, created for good works and ordained to walk in them.

I am a chosen generation, a royal priesthood, a holy nation and a peculiar people to show forth Your praise in the entire earth, Lord.

Ephesians 2:8-10
1 Peter 2:9

Other Books by
Billy Joe Daugherty

When Life Throws You a Curve

Led by the Spirit

Faith Power

Building Stronger Marriages and Families:
Making Your House a Home

Demonstration of the Gospel

Killing the Giant of Debt

You Can Be Healed

Absolute Victory

This New Life

Books by Sharon Daugherty

Called By His Side

Walking in the Fruit of the Spirit

Avoiding Deception

For more information about the ministry
or to receive a product catalog, you may contact:
Victory Christian Center
7700 South Lewis Avenue
Tulsa, OK 74136
(918) 491-7700

ABOUT THE AUTHOR

Billy Joe Daugherty is the pastor of Victory Christian Center in Tulsa, Oklahoma. Present ministry outreaches include a daily radio and television ministry; monthly crusades in government-subsidized housing projects in the Tulsa area; and crusades held in other nations.

Victory Christian Center, established in 1981, operates Victory Christian School, Victory Bible Institute, and the World Missions Training Center. Other Victory Bible Institutes have been established in 21 nations.

Billy Joe has authored several books including *Faith Power, Absolute Victory, This New Life, The Demonstration of the Gospel, Led By the Spirit*, and most recently, *When Life Throws You a Curve.*

Billy Joe and his wife, Sharon, were married in 1973, and have four children: Sarah, Ruth, John and Paul.

Victory Christian Center
7700 South Lewis Avenue
Tulsa, OK 74136-7700